E S T A T E   P U B L

LINCOLN

C000016236

Nettleham **16**

17 Sudbrooke

Reepham
4
Cherry Willingham

6 LINCOLN **7**

16 Skellingthorpe

5

Birchwood
8   Boultham **9**
Moor

New
10 Boultham **11**
Canwick

14 Washingborough

15 Branston

12 North
Hykeham

13

15 Bracebridge
Heath

17 Waddington

ROAD MAP	page **2−3**
ENLARGED CENTRE	page **5**
STREET INDEX	page **18**

Every effort has been made to verify
the accuracy of information in this
book but the publishers cannot accept
responsibility for expense or loss
caused by an error or omission.
Information that will be of assistance
to the user of the maps will be welcomed.

The representation on these maps of a
road, track or path is no evidence of the
existence of a right of way.

Car Park	🄿
Public Convenience	🄲
Place of Worship	✚
One-way Street	→
Pedestrianized	▨
Post Office	●

Scale of street plans 4 inches to 1 mile
Unless otherwise stated

Street plans prepared and published by ESTATE PUBLICATIONS, Bridewell House, TENTERDEN, KENT.
The Publishers acknowledge the co-operation of the local authorities
of towns represented in this atlas.

Ordnance Survey® This product includes mapping data licensed from Ordnance Survey®
with the permission of the Controller of Her Majesty's Stationery Office.

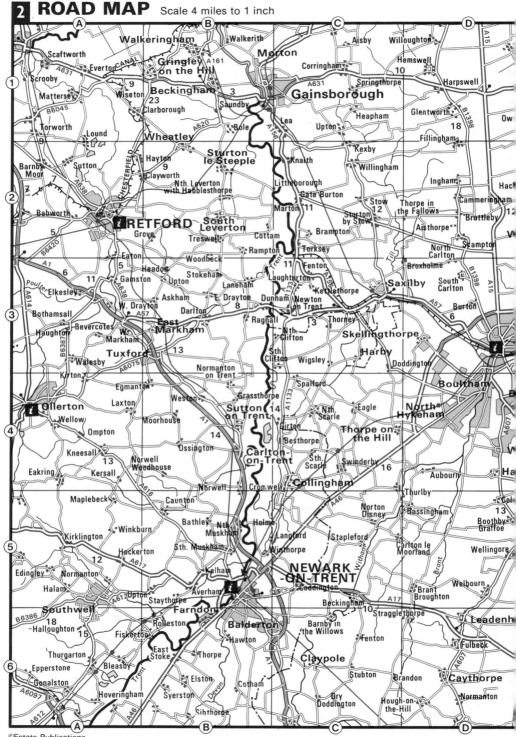

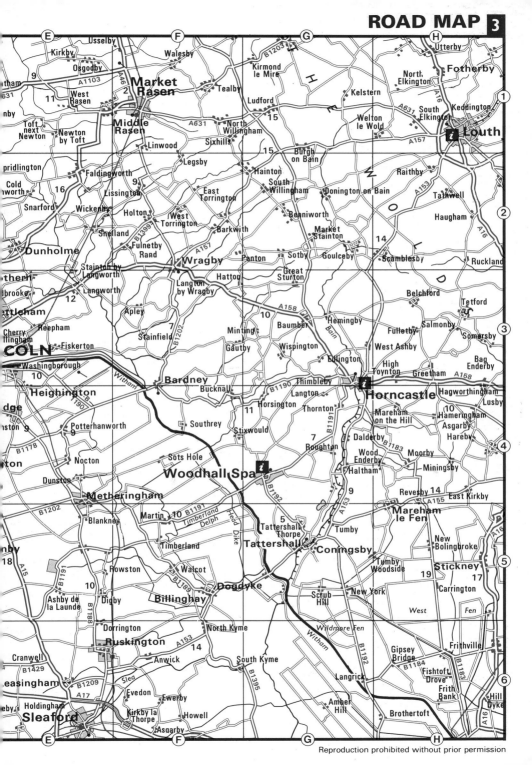

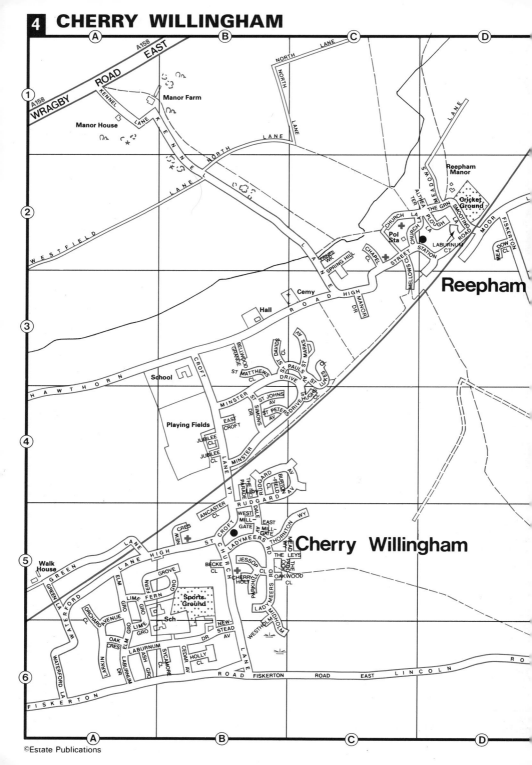

4 CHERRY WILLINGHAM

Reepham

Cherry Willingham

©Estate Publications

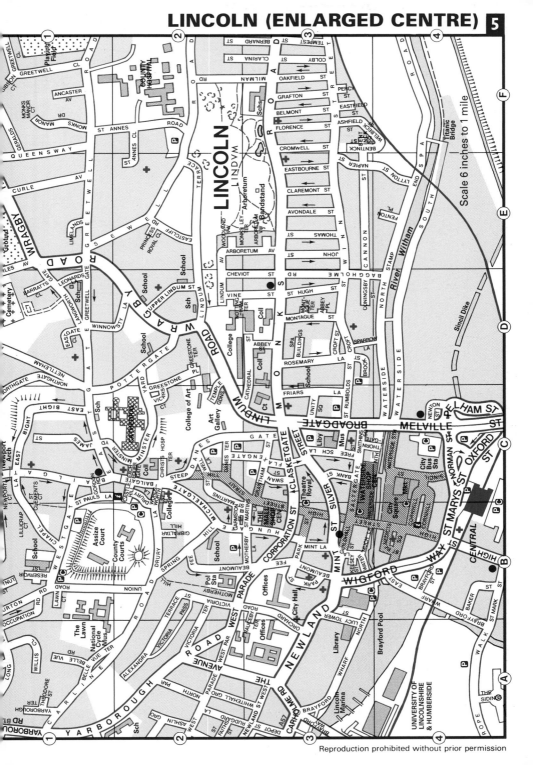

Scale 6 inches to 1 mile

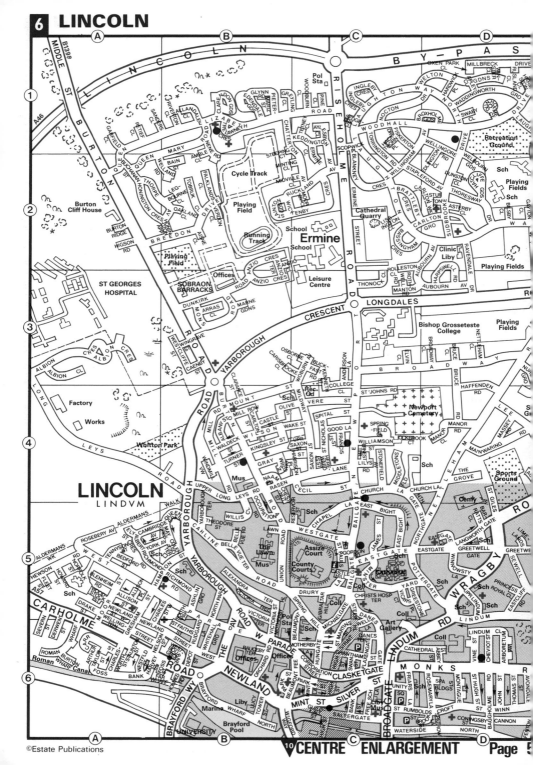

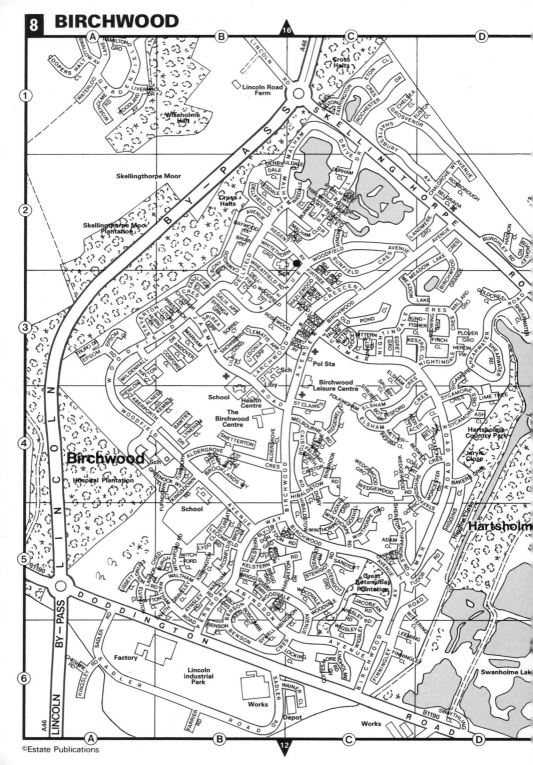

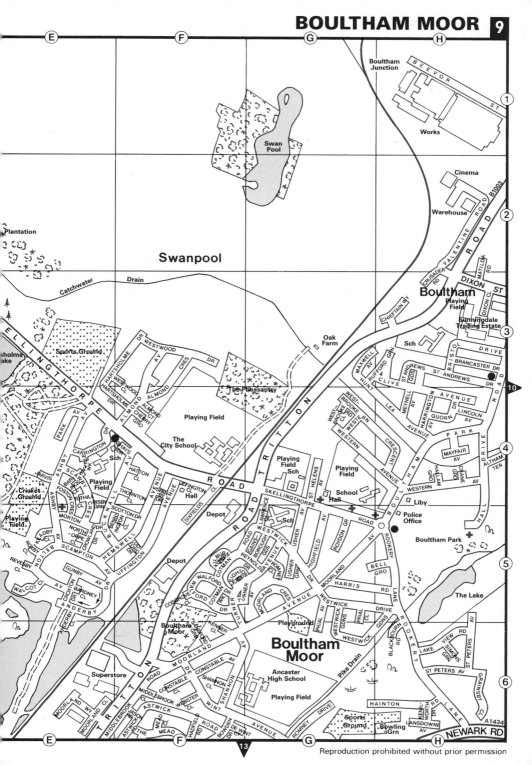

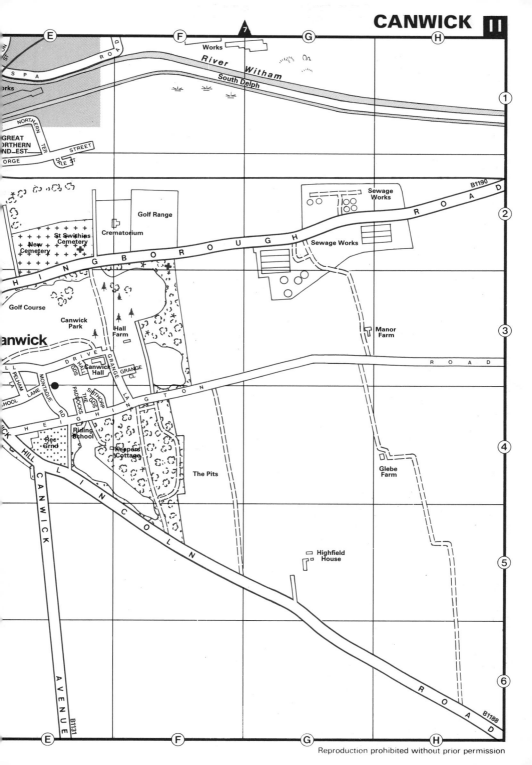

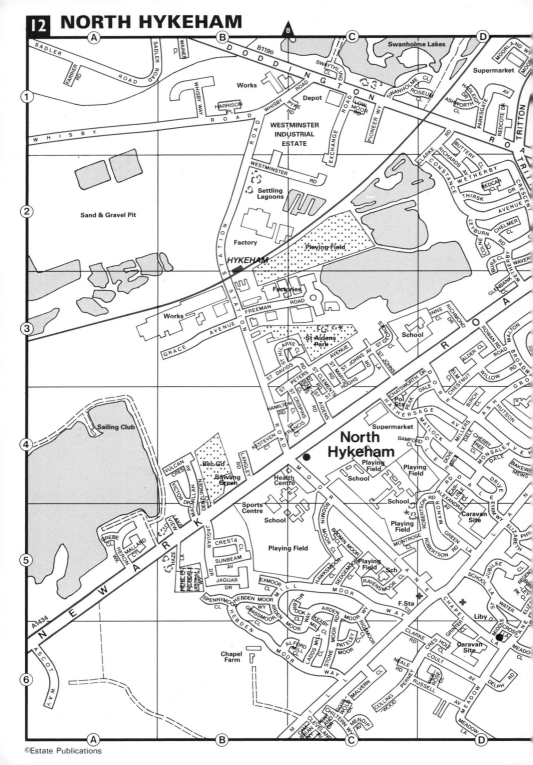

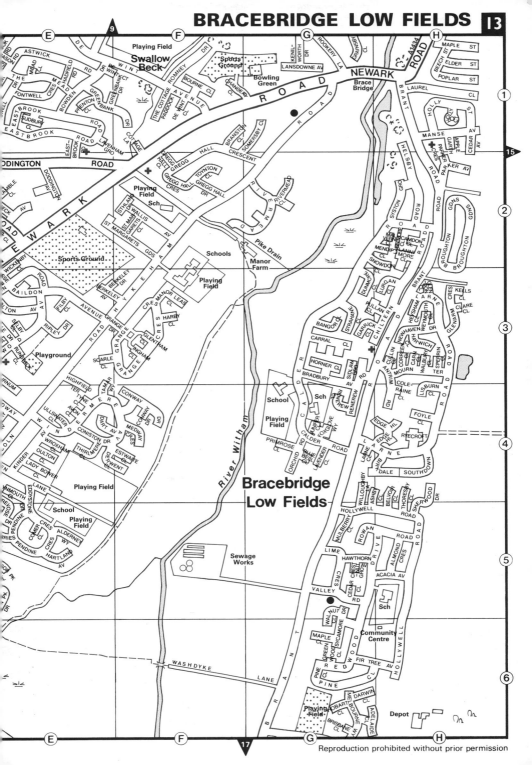

Washingborough

Heighington

Washingborough Fen

The Longstongs

The Viking Way

River Witham

North Delph

South Delph

Sandy Furze Farm

NEWCOT LA

HAWTHORN CL

POTTERHANWORTH

Rec Gd

Rec Gd

WASHINGBOROUGH ROAD

SHEEPWASH LANE

Heath Farm

Meadows Lodge

Manor Farm

ROYAL OAK LA

Schools

Playing Field

THE ORCHARD

HILL CROFT

CHURCH

LINCOLN ROAD MAIN ROAD

B1190

FERRY LA

HEIGHINGTON

CANWICK ROAD

CHURCH HILL

CLIFF LANE

WELLSYKES

STATION ROAD

©Estate Publications

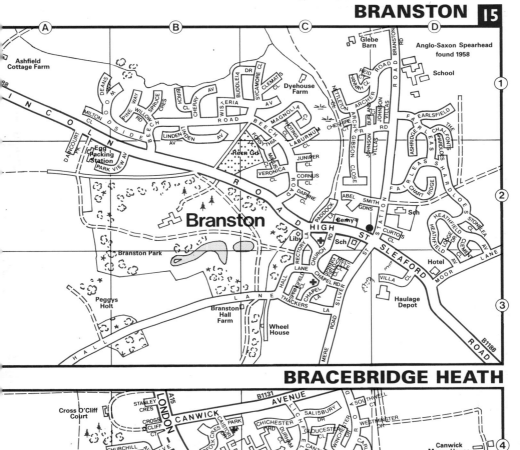

BRACEBRIDGE HEATH

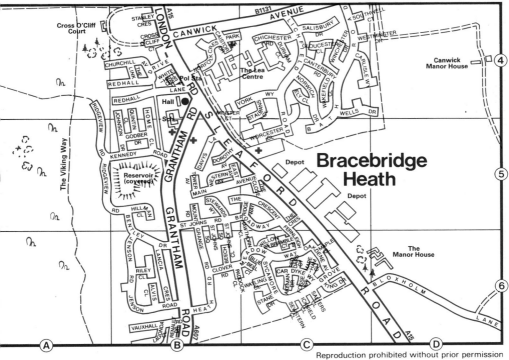

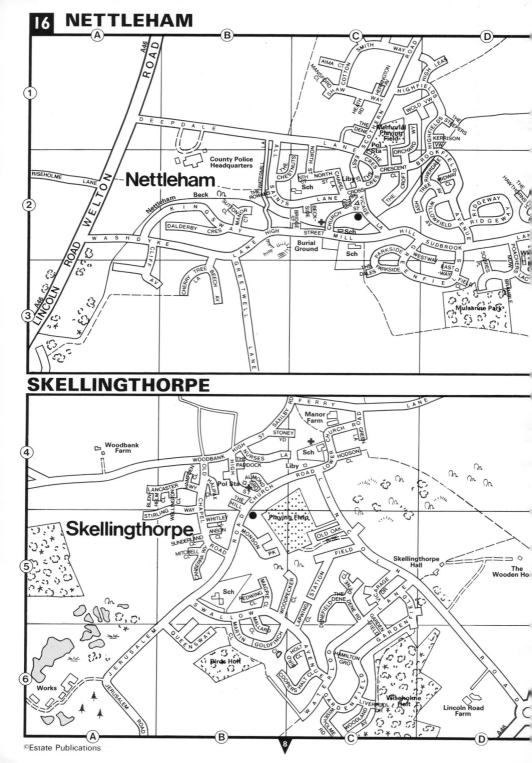

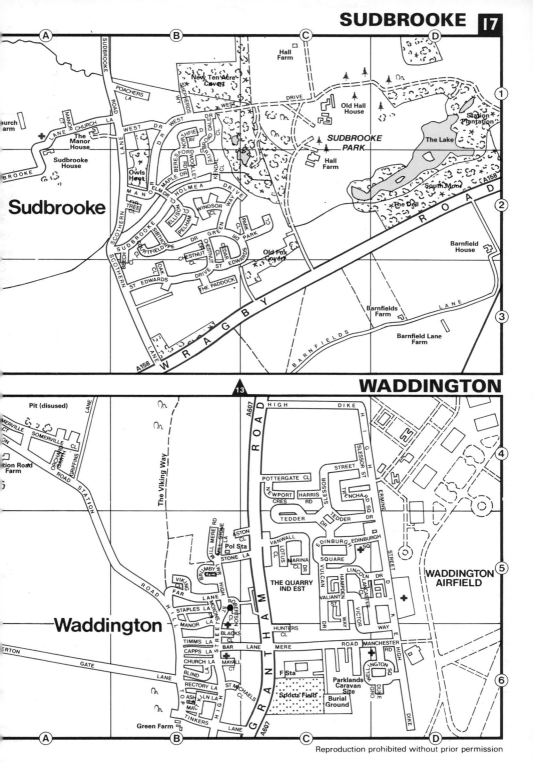

WADDINGTON

The Index includes some names for which there is insufficient space on the maps. These names are preceded by an * and are followed by the nearest adjoining thoroughfare.

Abbey Pl. LN2	5 D3
Abbey St. LN2	5 D3
*Abbeyfield Ho,	
Woburn Av. LN1	6 C3
Abbot St. LN5	10 C2
Abel Smith Gdns. LN4	15 C2
Aberporth Dri. LN6	8 A4
Abingdon Av. LN6	8 B5
Abingdon Clo. LN6	8 B6
Acacia Av. LN5	13 H5
Acer Clo. LN6	8 C4
Acer Ct. LN6	8 C4
Adam Clo. LN6	8 C5
Addison Dri. LN5	7 E3
Adelaide St. LN5	13 G6
Aima Ct. LN2	16 C1
Aisne Clo. LN1	6 B2
Akeman Dri. LN4	15 C6
Alabala Clo. LN4	14 C2
Alabala La. LN4	14 E3
Albany St. LN1	6 B4
Albany Ter. LN5	10 B6
Albert Cres. LN1	6 A5
Albion Clo. LN1	6 A3
Albion Cres. LN1	6 A3
Alconberry Clo. LN6	8 B5
Alder Clo. LN6	12 D3
Aldergrove Clo. LN6	8 B4
Aldergrove Cres. LN6	8 B4
Aldermans Walk. LN1	6 A5
Alderney Way. LN6	13 E5
Alexandra Av. LN6	12 D4
Alexandra Ter. LN1	5 A2
Alford Mill Clo. LN6	12 B6
Alfred St. LN5	10 B2
All Saints La. LN2	16 B2
Allandale Clo. LN1	6 B1
*Allandale Vw,	
Allandale Clo. LN1	6 B1
Allenby Rd. LN2	7 G6
Allison Pl. LN1	6 A5
Allison St. LN1	6 A5
Almond Av,	
Heighington. LN4	14 E4
Almond Av,	
Swanpool. LN6	9 F4
Almond Ct. LN6	9 F4
Almond Cres,	
Heighington. LN4	14 E4
Almond Cres,	
Swanpool LN6	9 F4
Almond Cres,	
Waddington. LN5	13 H5
Almond Gro. LN6	16 B4
Alness Clo. LN6	8 A4
Altham Ter. LN5	10 A4
Althea Ter. LN3	4 D2
Alvis Clo. LN4	15 B6
Amble Clo. LN1	6 B2
Ancaster Av. LN2	5 F1
Ancaster Clo. LN3	4 B5
Anchor St. LN5	10 B2
Anderby Clo. LN6	9 E6
Anderby Dri. LN6	9 E5
Anderson La. LN1	6 C3
Andover Clo. LN6	8 B3
Antrim Rd. LN5	13 H3
Anzio Clo. LN1	6 B2
Anzio Cres. LN1	6 B2
Anzio Ter. LN1	6 B2
Apley Clo. LN2	6 D1
Apple Clo. LN4	14 E4
Apple Garth. LN5	13 H1
Arabis Clo. LN2	7 F1
Arboretum Av. LN2	5 E2
Arboretum View. LN2	5 E3
Archer Rd. LN4	15 C1
Archer St. LN5	10 C2
Arden Moor Way. LN6	12 B5
Arlington Ct. LN4	14 B2
Arras Clo. LN1	6 B3
Arthur St. LN5	10 D2
Arthur Taylor St. LN1	6 A6
Ascot Way. LN6	12 A6
Ash Clo. LN6	8 D4
Ash Gro,	
Cherry Willingham. LN3	4 A6
Ash Gro,	
North Hykeham. LN6	12 D4
Ash La. LN5	17 B6
Ash Tree Av. LN2	16 D2
Ashby Av. LN6	9 E4
Ashby Clo. LN5	13 G4
Ashfield St. LN2	5 F3
Ashlin Gro. LN1	5 A2
Ashridge. LN4	15 D1
Ashtons Ct. LN5	10 B2
Ashworth Clo. LN6	12 D1
Aster Clo. LN2	7 F1
Asterby Clo. LN2	6 D2
Aston Clo. LN5	17 C5
Astral Way. LN6	12 B5
Astwick Rd. LN6	13 E1
Atwater Clo. LN2	7 G2
Atwater Gro. LN2	7 G2
Aubourn Av. LN2	6 D3
Auden Clo. LN2	6 D4
Austen Walk. LN2	7 F3
Avocet Clo. LN6	8 C3
Avon Clo. LN6	13 E4
Avondale. LN6	12 B5
Avondale St. LN2	5 E3
Aylesby Clo. LN1	6 C1
Aynsley Rd. LN6	8 B5
Azalea Rd. LN2	7 F1
Back La. LN4	14 E4
Baggholme Rd. LN2	5 D3
Baildon Av. LN6	13 E3
Bailgate. LN1	5 C1
Bain St. LN1	6 B2
Baker St. LN5	5 B4
Bakers Cres. LN6	8 D4
Bakewell Mews. LN6	12 D4
*Balmoral Ho,	
Thurlby Cres. LN2	7 E2
Bamford Clo. LN6	12 D4
Bangor Clo. LN5	13 G3
Bank St. LN2	5 C3
Bar La. LN5	17 B6
Bardney Clo. LN4	9 E5
Bargate. LN5	10 B4
Barings Clo. LN6	9 E4
Barkston Gdns. LN2	7 E2
Barleyfield Clo. LN4	14 C3
Barnfields La. LN2	17 C3
Barratts Clo. LN2	5 D1
Bassingham Cres. LN2	6 C2
Bath Rd. LN4	15 C5
Bathurst St. LN2	7 G6
Bawtry Clo. LN6	8 B4
Baywood Clo. LN6	8 B2
Beaufort Clo. LN2	7 G2
Beaufort Rd. LN2	7 G2
Beaumont Fee. LN1	5 B2
Beck La. LN4	14 E3
Becke Clo. LN3	4 B5
Becket Clo. LN4	14 D2
Beckside. LN2	16 C2
Bedford St. LN1	6 A5
Beech Av. LN2	16 B3
Beech Clo,	
Bracebridge Heath. LN4	15 B6
Beech Clo, Sudbrooke. LN2	17 B2
Beech Rd. LN4	15 C1
Beech St. LN5	10 B6
Beevor St. LN6	10 A1
Belgrave Ct. LN4	14 B2
Belgravia Clo. LN6	8 D2
Bell Gro. LN6	9 H5
Bell St. LN5	10 B3
Belle Vue Rd. LN1	5 A1
Belle Vue Ter. LN1	5 A1
Bellflower Clo. LN2	7 F1
Bells Meadow. LN4	14 E4
Bellwood Grange. LN3	4 B3
Belmont St. LN2	5 F3
Belton Av. LN6	9 E5
Belton Park Dri. LN6	13 E5
Belton Sq. LN4	14 E4
Belvoir Clo. LN5	13 H4
Belvoir Sq. LN4	14 E4
Bennington Clo. LN6	9 F5
Benson Clo. LN6	8 B6
Benson Cres. LN6	8 B6
Bentinck Sq. LN2	5 F3
Bentinck St. LN2	5 F3
Bentley Dri. LN4	15 B5
Beresford Dri. LN2	17 B2
Berkeley Av. LN6	13 E3
Berkeley Ct. LN4	14 B2
Berkeley Dri. LN6	13 E3
Bernard St. LN2	5 F3
Beswick Clo. LN6	8 D4
Betula Gro. LN6	8 D4
Beverley Gro. LN6	12 D3
Bilsby Clo. LN2	6 D2
Binbrook Clo. LN6	8 C4
Birch Clo,	
Branston. LN4	15 B1
Birch Clo,	
North Hykeham. LN6	12 D4
Birchwood Av. LN6	8 C3
Birchwood Cres. LN6	8 D2
Birchwood Grange. LN6	8 D2
Bird Holt Clo. LN6	16 C6
Birkdale. LN5	13 H4
Birkdale Clo. LN4	14 E2
Bishop Kings Ct. LN5	10 C3
Bishops Rd. LN2	7 F4
Bitten Way. LN6	8 C3
Blackbourn Rd. LN6	9 H6
Blacks Clo. LN5	17 B6
Blacksmith La. LN4	14 E3
Blackthorn Clo. LN2	7 F1
Blankney Cres. LN2	6 C2
Blenheim Clo. LN6	16 A4
Blenheim Rd. LN1	6 A5
Blind La. LN5	17 B6
Bloxholm La. LN5	15 D6
Bluebell Clo. LN5	13 G4
Bluebell Ct. LN4	15 C6
Blydon Clo. LN6	8 B5
Blydon Gro. LN6	8 B5
Blydon Rd. LN6	8 B5
Bodmin Moor Clo. LN6	12 C5
Bolton Av. LN6	13 E3
Boscombe Clo. LN6	8 B5
Boswell Dri. LN6	13 E1
Boswell Gro. LN6	13 E1
Bottesford Clo. LN6	8 C4
Boultham Av. LN5	10 B2
Boultham Park Rd. LN6	10 A3
Boundary St. LN5	10 B5
Bourne Clo. LN6	13 F1
Bowden Dri. LN6	13 E1
Bradbury Av. LN5	13 G3
Bramble Clo. LN6	13 E2
Bramble Ct,	
Bracebridge Heath. LN4	15 C6
Bramble Ct,	
Nettleham. LN2	16 D3
Bramley Clo. LN5	13 E1
Brancaster Dri. LN6	10 A3
Branston Clo. LN6	13 F1
Branston Rd,	
Branston. LN4	15 D1
Branston Rd,	
Heighington. LN4	14 ?
Brant Rd. LN5	13 ?
Brattleby Cres. LN2	6 ?
Brayford St. LN5	5 ?
Brayford Way. LN5	5 ?
Brayford Wharf East. LN5	5 ?
Brayford Wharf North. LN1	5 ?
Breedon Dri. LN1	6 ?
Briar Clo. LN6	8 ?
Bridge St. LN2	16 ?
Brigg Clo. LN6	8 ?
Brigg Gro. LN6	8 ?
Brisbane Clo. LN5	13 ?
Bristol Dri. LN6	10 ?
Broad Dale Clo. LN2	17 ?
Broadgate. LN2	5 ?
Broadway,	
Bracebridge Heath. LN4	15 ?
Broadway, Lincoln. LN2	6 ?
Broadway,	
North Hykeham. LN6	12 ?
Broadway Clo. LN2	6 ?
Brook St. LN2	5 ?
Brookfield Av. LN2	16 ?
Brooklands Clo. LN6	8 ?
Brooklands Way. LN6	8 ?
Brough Clo. LN6	8 ?
Broughton Gdns. LN5	13 ?
Browning Dri. LN2	7 ?
Broxholme Gdns. LN2	6 ?
Bruce Clo. LN2	6 ?
Bruce Rd. LN2	6 ?
Brumby Cres. LN5	17 ?
Buchanan St. LN1	6 ?
Buckfast Rd. LN1	6 ?
*Buckingham Ho,	
Weldon Gdns. LN2	6 ?
Bucknall Av. LN6	9 ?
Buddleia Dri. LN4	15 ?
Bullingham Rd. LN2	7 ?
Bunkers Hill. LN2	7 ?
Bure Clo. LN6	12 ?
Burghley Clo. LN6	8 ?
Burghley Park Clo. LN6	12 ?
Burghley Sq. LN4	14 ?
Burghley Rd. LN6	8 ?
Burland Ct, Branston. LN4	15 ?
Burland Ct,	
Washingborough. LN4	14 ?
Burmoor Clo. LN6	8 ?
Burns Gdns. LN2	7 ?
Burnside Clo. LN2	7 ?
Burton Mews. LN4	14 ?
Burton Ridge. LN1	6 ?
Burton Rd. LN1	5 ?
Burton Wharf. LN1	6 ?
Burtonfield Clo. LN3	4 ?
Burwell Clo. LN2	7 ?
Butchers La. LN4	14 ?
Buttermere Clo. LN6	8 ?
Buttery Clo. LN6	12 ?
Byron Av. LN2	6 ?
Cabourne Av. LN2	7 ?
Cabourne Ct. LN2	7 ?
Cadwell Clo. LN6	8 ?
Caenby St. LN1	6 ?
Caistor Clo. LN6	8 ?
Caistor Dri. LN4	15 ?
Caistor Rd. LN6	8 ?
Calder Rd. LN5	13 ?
Cambrian Way. LN6	12 ?
Cambridge Av. LN1	6 ?
Cambridge Dri. LN4	14 ?
Camdon Clo. LN5	13 ?
Camwood Av. LN6	8 ?
*Canberra Sq,	
Wellington Sq. LN5	17 ?
Canberra Way. LN6	16 ?
Cannon St. LN2	5 ?

Canterbury Dri. LN4 — 14 D3
Canterbury Rd. LN4 — 15 C4
Canwick Av,
Bracebridge Heath. LN4 — 15 B4
Canwick Av,
Canwick. LN4 — 11 E4
Canwick Hill. LN4 — 11 E4
Canwick Rd. LN5 — 10 C1
Canwick Rd. LN4 — 14 B3
Capps La. LN5 — 17 B6
Car Dyke Way. LN4 — 15 C6
Cardinal Clo. LN2 — 7 F4
Carholme Rd. LN1 — 5 A3
Carisbrooke Clo. LN1 — 6 C4
Carline Rd. LN1 — 5 A1
Carlisle Clo. LN6 — 12 D4
Carlisle Way. LN4 — 15 C4
Carlton Blvd. LN2 — 7 G4
Carlton Gro. LN2 — 6 D2
Carlton Mews. LN4 — 14 D3
Carlton St. LN1 — 6 B4
Carlton Walk. LN2 — 6 D2
Carlyle Walk. LN2 — 7 E4
Carn Clo. LN5 — 13 H3
Carr St. LN1 — 6 A6
Carral Clo. LN5 — 13 G3
Carrington Dri. LN6 — 9 E4
Castle Hill. LN1 — 5 C2
Castle St. LN1 — 6 B4
Cathedral St. LN2 — 5 C3
Cathedral Vw Ct,
Cabourne St. LN2 — 7 E2
Cavendish Mews. LN4 — 14 D2
Cecil Mews. LN1 — 5 B1
Cecil St. LN1 — 5 B1
Cedar Av, Bracebridge
Low Fields. LN5 — 13 H1
Cedar Av,
Cherry Willingham. LN3 — 4 B6
Cedar Clo, Bracebridge
Low Fields. LN5 — 13 G5
Cedar Clo, Sudbrooke. LN2 — 17 B2
Centaur Rd. LN6 — 10 A1
Centurion Rd. LN5 — 10 B2
Chalgrove Way. LN6 — 8 D2
Chancery Clo. LN6 — 13 F1
Chapel Clo. LN3 — 4 C2
Chapel La,
Branston. LN4 — 15 C3
Chapel La,
Heighington. LN4 — 14 D4
Chapel La, Lincoln. LN1 — 5 B1
Chapel La,
Nettleham. LN2 — 16 C2
Chapel La,
North Hykeham. LN6 — 12 D5
Chapel Rd. LN4 — 15 C3
Chaplin St. LN5 — 10 C2
Charles St. LN5 — 10 C2
Charles St West. LN1 — 6 A5
Charlesworth St. LN1 — 6 A6
Chart Ridge. LN4 — 15 D2
Chatsworth Clo. LN2 — 7 F1
Chatterton Av. LN1 — 6 B1
Chaucer Dri. LN2 — 7 F4
Chedburgh Clo. LN6 — 8 B5
Chedworth Clo. LN2 — 7 G2
Chedworth Rd. LN2 — 7 G2
Chelmer Clo. LN6 — 12 D2
Chelmsford St. LN5 — 10 C2
Chelsea Clo. LN6 — 8 C1
Cherry Av. LN4 — 15 B1
Cherry Gro. LN6 — 9 F4
Cherry Holt. LN3 — 4 B5
Cherry Tree Clo. LN6 — 12 D4
Cherry Tree La. LN2 — 16 B3
Cheshire Ct. LN4 — 15 C1
Cheshire Ho,
Woodhall Dri. LN6 — 6 D1
Cheshire Rd. LN6 — 8 A6
Chesney Rd. LN2 — 7 G2
Chester Clo. LN4 — 15 C1
Chestnut Clo. LN2 — 17 B2
Chestnut Dri. LN2 — 17 B2
Chestnut Gro. LN5 — 13 G5
Chestnut Rd. LN6 — 12 D3

Chestnut St. LN1 — 5 B1
*Cheviot Clo,
Cleveland Av. LN6 — 12 C6
Cheviot St. LN2 — 5 D2
Chichester Rd. LN4 — 15 C4
Chieftain Way. LN6 — 9 H3
Chiltern Rd. LN5 — 13 H3
Chiltern Way. LN6 — 12 C6
Chippendale Clo. LN6 — 8 C5
Chippendale Rd. LN6 — 8 C5
Chivenor Clo. LN6 — 8 B3
Christs Hospital Ter. LN2 — 5 C2
Church Dri. LN6 — 10 A2
Church Hill. LN4 — 14 B1
Church La,
Cherry Willingham. LN3 — 4 B5
Church La, Lincoln. LN2 — 5 C1
Church La,
Reepham. LN3 — 4 C2
Church La,
Sudbrooke. LN2 — 17 A1
Church La,
Waddington. LN5 — 17 B6
Church Rd, Branston. LN4 — 15 C3
Church Rd,
Skellingthorpe. LN6 — 16 B4
Church St. LN2 — 16 C2
Churchill Av. LN4 — 15 B4
Clarance St. LN1 — 6 B4
Clare Clo. LN5 — 13 H3
Claremont St. LN2 — 5 E3
Clarendon Ct. LN4 — 14 B2
Clarendon Gdns. LN1 — 6 B1
*Clarendon Vw,
Clarendon Gdns. LN1 — 6 B1
Clarina St. LN2 — 5 F3
Clarke Av. LN4 — 14 E4
Clarke Rd,
Boultham Moor. LN6 — 12 D1
Clarke Rd,
North Hykeham. LN6 — 12 C6
Clasketgate. LN2 — 5 C3
Clayton Rd. LN5 — 10 B5
Clematis App. LN6 — 8 B3
Clematis Clo. LN4 — 15 C1
Clement Clo. LN4 — 15 D2
Cleveland Av. LN6 — 12 C6
Cliff Av. LN2 — 16 A2
Cliff La. LN2 — 14 B3
Clifton St. LN5 — 10 D2
Clive Av. LN6 — 9 H3
Clover Rd. LN4 — 15 B6
Clumber St. LN5 — 10 B5
Coalport Clo. LN6 — 8 C4
Colby St. LN2 — 5 F3
Colegrave St. LN5 — 10 B4
Colenso Ter. LN1 — 6 B5
Coleraine Clo. LN5 — 13 H4
Coleridge Gdns. LN2 — 7 E2
Coleridge Grn. LN2 — 7 F3
College Clo. LN1 — 6 C3
Collingwood. LN6 — 12 C6
Colne Clo. LN6 — 12 D2
Comer Clo. LN6 — 13 E5
Coningsby Cres. LN4 — 10 C6
Coningsby St. LN2 — 5 D3
Coniston Dri. LN6 — 13 E4
Connaught Ter. LN5 — 10 B6
Constable Av. LN6 — 9 F6
Constable Clo. LN6 — 9 F6
Constance Av. LN6 — 12 D2
Conway Dri. LN6 — 13 F4
*Coopers Clo,
Cotton Smith Way. LN2 — 16 C1
Coopers Halt Clo. LN6 — 16 C6
Cornhill. LN5 — 5 B4
Cornus Clo. LN4 — 15 C2
Cornwallis Rd. LN3 — 7 G6
Corporation St. LN2 — 5 B3
Correen Clo. LN5 — 13 H3
Cosford Clo. LN6 — 8 B3
Cosgrove Clo. LN6 — 9 F5
Cotman Rd. LN6 — 9 F5
Cotman Walk. LN6 — 9 F5
Cotswold Clo. LN6 — 12 C6
Cottage La. LN6 — 13 F1
Cottesmore Rd. LN6 — 8 C6

Cottingham Dri. LN2 — 7 E3
Cotton Smith Way. LN2 — 16 C1
Coulson St. LN6 — 10 A2
Coult Av. LN6 — 12 D6
Courtfield Clo. LN2 — 17 B2
Cowper Dri. LN2 — 7 F3
Cranbourne Mews. LN4 — 14 D1
Crane Gro. LN6 — 10 A4
Cranwell St. LN5 — 10 B3
*Craven Mews,
Craven St. LN5 — 10 B3
Craven St. LN5 — 10 B3
Crescent Clo. LN2 — 16 C2
Cresta Clo. LN6 — 12 B5
Croft La. LN3 — 4 B3
Croft St. LN2 — 5 D3
Crofton Clo. LN3 — 7 G6
Crofton Dri. LN3 — 7 G5
Crofton Rd. LN3 — 7 G5
Cromwell Clo. LN4 — 14 A2
Cromwell St. LN2 — 5 F3
Cross La. LN6 — 12 D6
Cross O'Cliff Clo. LN5 — 10 C5
Cross O'Cliff Ct. LN4 — 15 B4
Cross O'Cliff Hill. LN5 — 10 B4
Cross Spencer St. LN5 — 10 B3
Cross St, Lincoln. LN5 — 10 C3
Cross St, Nettleham. LN2 — 16 C2
Crowland Dri. LN6 — 9 E5
Croxton Dri. LN6 — 9 E5
Crusader Rd. LN6 — 10 A3
Cullin Clo. LN5 — 13 H3
Curle Av. LN2 — 5 E1
Curtis Dri. LN4 — 14 D4
Curtois Clo. LN4 — 15 D2
Curzon Mews. LN4 — 14 D2
Cydonia App. LN6 — 8 B3
D'Aincourt Pk. LN4 — 15 A2
Dalderby Cres. LN2 — 16 B2
Dale Av. LN3 — 4 B5
Dale St. LN5 — 11 E2
Danes Gate. LN2 — 5 C2
Danes Ter. LN2 — 5 C2
Daniel Cres. LN4 — 14 D3
Daniel Gdns. LN4 — 14 D3
Daphne Clo. LN4 — 15 C2
Dart Av. LN6 — 13 E4
Darwin Clo. LN5 — 13 G6
Davys La. LN4 — 15 B5
De Wint Av. LN6 — 9 F6
De Wint Clo. LN6 — 13 F1
De Wint Ct. LN6 — 13 E1
Deacon Rd. LN2 — 7 F4
Dean Rd. LN2 — 7 F4
Deans Way. LN4 — 15 A1
Deepdale La. LN4 — 16 A1
Dellfield Av. LN6 — 8 B3
Dellfield Clo. LN6 — 8 B3
Dellfield Ct. LN6 — 8 B3
Deloraine Ct. LN4 — 14 B2
Delph Rd. LN6 — 12 D6
Denbydale Clo. LN6 — 8 B2
Dene Clo. LN6 — 16 C5
Dene Rd. LN6 — 16 C5
Denefield. LN6 — 16 C5
Denzingen Clo. LN6 — 12 B5
Depot St. LN1 — 5 A3
Derby St. LN5 — 10 B4
Derwent Clo. LN6 — 13 E4
Derwent St. LN1 — 6 A6
Devon St. LN2 — 7 F6
Digby Clo. LN6 — 8 C4
Dixon Clo. LN5 — 10 A3
Dixon St. LN5 — 10 A3
Dixon Way. LN5 — 10 B3
Doddington Av. LN6 — 13 E2
Doddington Rd. LN6 — 8 A5
Dore Av. LN6 — 12 D3
Dorothy Av. LN4 — 15 B5
Dorset St. LN2 — 7 F6
Doulton Clo. LN6 — 8 D4
Dove Dale. LN6 — 12 D4
Dowding Rd. LN3 — 7 H5
Drake Av. LN1 — 6 A5
Drake St. LN1 — 6 A5
Drury La. LN1 — 5 B2

Dryden Av. LN2 — 7 E3
Dukes Gro. LN5 — 17 D6
Dunford Rd. LN5 — 10 D2
Dunholme Ct. LN2 — 6 D1
Dunkirk Rd. LN1 — 6 B3
Dunlop St. LN5 — 10 C3
Dunmore Clo. LN5 — 13 G3
Dunston Clo. LN2 — 6 D2
Durham Clo,
Birchwood. LN6 — 8 C2
Durham Clo,
Bracebridge Heath. LN4 — 15 C4
Durham Cres. LN4 — 14 D2
Earls Dri. LN6 — 10 A3
Earlsfield. LN4 — 15 D1
East Av. LN4 — 15 B5
East Bight. LN2 — 5 C1
East Croft. LN3 — 4 B4
East Liberty. LN2 — 7 F5
East Millgate. LN3 — 4 B5
East St. LN2 — 16 C2
Eastbourne St. LN2 — 5 E3
Eastbrook Rd. LN6 — 13 E1
Eastcliff Rd. LN2 — 5 E2
Eastfield St. LN2 — 5 F3
Eastgate. LN2 — 5 C1
Eastgate Clo. LN2 — 5 D1
Eastleigh Clo. LN6 — 8 B3
Eastway. LN2 — 16 D3
Ebony Gro. LN6 — 8 B2
Eddystone Dri. LN6 — 13 E4
Edendale Gdns. LN1 — 6 B1
*Edendale Vw,
Edendale Gdns. LN1 — 6 B1
Edge Hill. LN5 — 13 H4
Edinburgh Sq. LN5 — 17 C5
Edlington Clo. LN2 — 6 D2
Edna St. LN5 — 10 C3
Edward Barker Rd. LN4 — 14 E4
Edward St. LN5 — 10 B3
Egerton Rd. LN2 — 7 E4
Egret Gro. LN6 — 8 C3
Elder St. LN5 — 10 B6
Eleanor Clo. LN5 — 10 B5
Elizabeth Av. LN6 — 12 D5
Ellesmere Av. LN2 — 7 G6
Elliot Rd. LN5 — 10 D2
Ellison Clo. LN2 — 17 B2
Ellison St. LN5 — 10 B6
Elm Clo. LN6 — 12 D3
Elm Dri. LN2 — 17 B2
Elm Gro. LN3 — 4 A5
Elmwood Clo. LN6 — 8 C3
Elsham Clo. LN6 — 8 C3
Elsham Cres. LN6 — 8 C3
Elvin Clo. LN2 — 6 C3
Elvington Clo. LN6 — 8 A5
Elvington Rd. LN6 — 8 A5
Ely Clo. LN4 — 15 C4
Ely St. LN1 — 6 A5
Enderby Clo. LN4 — 14 A2
Ennerdale Clo. LN6 — 8 C2
Epsom Clo. LN6 — 8 A3
Epsom Rd. LN6 — 8 A3
*Epworth Vw,
Clarendon Gdns. LN1 — 6 B1
Ermine Clo. LN1 — 6 C1
Ermine Clo, Lincoln. LN1 — 6 C2
Ermine St,
Waddington. LN5 — 17 D4
Ernel Walk. LN3 — 4 C2
Ernest Ter. LN1 — 6 C4
*Escombe Vw,
Sanders Clo. LN1 — 6 A1
Esk Clo. LN6 — 13 E2
Estwaite Clo. LN6 — 13 F4
Eton Clo. LN6 — 8 C1
Eton Rd. LN4 — 14 C2
Euston Clo. LN6 — 8 D1
Eve Gdns. LN4 — 14 D3
Ewart St. LN5 — 10 B4
Exchange Rd. LN6 — 12 C1
Exchequer Gate. LN2 — 5 C2
Exeter Clo. LN4 — 14 E2
Exmoor Clo. LN6 — 12 C6
Eyam Way. LN6 — 12 D5

19

Fairfax St. LN5 — 10 B5
Fairfield St. LN2 — 7 E6
Fairleas. LN4 — 15 D1
Falcon View. LN6 — 8 C3
Faldingworth Clo. LN6 — 8 C4
Falklands Clo. LN1 — 6 B2
Far La. LN5 — 17 B5
Far Wharf. LN1 — 5 A3
Farrier Rd. LN6 — 8 B6
Farrington Clo. LN6 — 8 C1
Farrington Cres. LN6 — 8 C1
Favell Rd. LN4 — 14 B2
Fawsley Clo. LN2 — 7 H2
Featherby Pl. LN5 — 10 B3
Fen La. LN6 — 13 E4
Fen Rd, Heighington. LN4 — 14 F4
Fen Rd, Washingborough. LN4 — 14 C1
Fen View. LN4 — 14 F4
Fenton Pl. LN2 — 5 E4
Fern Gro. LN3 — 4 A5
Fernleigh Av. LN4 — 15 C6
Ferry La, Skellingthorpe. LN6 — 16 C4
Ferry La, Washingborough. LN4 — 14 B1
Field Clo. LN2 — 16 D3
Filby Clo. LN6 — 13 E3
Finch Clo. LN6 — 8 D3
Finningley Clo. LN6 — 8 C6
Finningley Rd. LN6 — 8 C6
Fir Tree Av. LN5 — 13 G6
Fir Tree Clo. LN2 — 17 B2
Firth Rd. LN5 — 10 B1
Firtree Av. LN6 — 8 C3
Fiskerton Dri. LN2 — 6 C1
Fiskerton Rd, Cherry Willingham. LN3 — 4 A6
Fiskerton Rd, Reepham. LN3 — 4 D2
Fiskerton Rd East. LN3 — 4 B6
Flaxengate. LN2 — 5 C3
Fleet St. LN1 — 6 A5
Florence St. LN2 — 5 F3
Folkingham Clo. LN6 — 8 C4
Fontwell Cres. LN6 — 13 E1
Forsythia Clo. LN4 — 15 C2
Foss Bank. LN1 — 6 A6
Foss St. LN1 — 6 B6
Fosse Ct. LN4 — 15 C6
Fosse Dri. LN6 — 13 E3
Foster St. LN5 — 10 B2
Foston Cres. LN6 — 9 E4
Foxglove Way. LN5 — 13 G4
Foyle Clo. LN5 — 13 H4
Francis St, Bracebridge. LN5 — 10 B6
Francis St, Lincoln. LN1 — 6 C4
Frank St. LN5 — 10 B3
Frank Swaby Ct. LN5 — 10 B5
Frank Wright Ct. LN2 — 7 F3
Frederick St. LN1 — 7 F6
Free School La. LN2 — 5 C3
Freeman Rd. LN6 — 12 B3
Friars La. LN2 — 5 C3
Fulmar Rd. LN6 — 8 C3
Fulstow Rd. LN2 — 7 E1
Furndown.Ct LN6 — 8 B4

Gail Gro. LN4 — 14 D3
Gainsborough Gdns. LN6 — 9 G5
Gardenfield. LN6 — 16 C6
Garfield Clo. LN1 — 6 A1
*Garfield Vw, Garfield Clo. LN1 — 6 A1
Garmston St. LN2 — 5 B2
Garratt Clo. LN4 — 14 D4
Garrick Clo. LN5 — 13 G3
Gaunt St. LN5 — 10 B2
Gayton Clo. LN2 — 6 D2
Geneva Av. LN2 — 7 E3
George St. LN5 — 11 E2
Geralds Clo. LN2 — 5 F1
Gerrard Mews. LN4 — 14 D2
Gibbeson St. LN5 — 10 B3
Gibraltar Hill. LN1 — 5 B2

Gibson Clo. LN4 — 15 C1
Gibson Ct. LN2 — 5 F1
*Gibson Ho, Roughton Ct. LN2 — 6 D1
Gildesburgh Rd. LN4 — 14 B2
Gleedale. LN6 — 12 D4
Glenarm Cres. LN5 — 13 H3
Glenbank Clo. LN6 — 12 D3
Glendon Clo. LN5 — 13 H3
Gleneagles Gro. LN4 — 14 D2
Glentham Clo. LN6 — 13 F3
Glenwood Gro. LN6 — 10 A3
Gloucester Clo. LN4 — 15 C4
Glynn Rd. LN1 — 6 B1
*Glynn Vw, Glynn Rd. LN1 — 6 B1
Godber Dri. LN4 — 15 B5
Goldcrest Clo. LN6 — 8 D3
Goldfinch Clo. LN6 — 16 B6
Goldsmith Walk. LN2 — 7 F2
Good La. LN1 — 6 C4
Gordon Rd. LN1 — 5 C1
Gothic Clo. LN6 — 8 D5
Goxhill Clo. LN6 — 8 C5
Goxhill Gro. LN6 — 8 C5
Grace Av. LN6 — 12 B3
Grace St. LN5 — 10 C2
Grafton St. LN2 — 5 F3
Grainsby Clo. LN6 — 9 H6
Grange Clo. LN4 — 11 F3
Grange Cres. LN6 — 13 F3
Grange Dri. LN6 — 13 E3
Grange La, Canwick. LN4 — 11 E3
Grange La, Heighington. LN4 — 14 D4
Grange Rd. LN4 — 15 B6
Granson Way. LN4 — 14 A2
Grantham Rd, Bracebridge Heath. LN4 — 15 B5
Grantham Rd, Waddington. LN5 — 17 C6
Grantham St. LN2 — 5 C3
Grasmere Way. LN6 — 8 C2
Grassmoor Clo. LN6 — 12 B5
Graveley Clo. LN6 — 8 B5
Gray St. LN1 — 6 B4
Great Northern Ter. LN5 — 10 D1
Grebe Clo. LN6 — 12 A5
Green La, Cherry Willingham. LN3 — 4 A5
Green La, New Boultham. LN6 — 10 A1
Green La, North Hykeham. LN6 — 12 D5
Green La, Skellingthorpe. LN6 — 16 C4
Green Way. LN2 — 17 B2
Greenbank Dri. LN6 — 13 E1
Greenfields. LN2 — 16 C2
Greenholme Clo. LN2 — 6 D1
Greenock Way. LN6 — 8 B4
Greenwood Clo. LN5 — 13 G6
Greestone Pl. LN2 — 5 D2
Greestone Ter. LN2 — 5 D2
Greetwell Clo. LN2 — 5 F1
Greetwell Gate. LN2 — 5 D1
Greetwell La. LN2 — 16 B3
Greetwell Pl. LN2 — 7 E5
Greetwell Rd. LN2 — 5 E1
Gregg Hall Clo. LN6 — 13 F2
Gregg Hall Dri. LN6 — 13 F2
Gregg Hall Cres. LN6 — 13 F2
Gresham St. LN1 — 6 A5
Gresley Dri. LN6 — 10 B3
*Grey Friars Pathway, Free School La. LN2 — 5 C3
Greyling Clo. LN1 — 6 C1
*Greyling Vw, Greyling Clo. LN1 — 6 C1
Griffins La. LN5 — 17 A4
Grinter Clo. LN6 — 12 D6
Grosvenor Av. LN6 — 8 C1
Grosvenor Mews. LN4 — 14 D2
Guildhall St. LN1 — 5 B3
Gunby Av. LN6 — 9 E5
Gynewell Gro. LN2 — 7 F2

Hackthorn Pl. LN2 — 6 C1
Haddon Clo. LN6 — 8 D2
Hadfield Rd. LN6 — 13 E1
Hadleigh Dri. LN6 — 12 D1
Haffenden Rd. LN2 — 6 D4
Hainton Rd. LN6 — 9 H6
Hale Clo. LN2 — 7 H2
Halifax Clo. LN6 — 16 B4
Hall Dri, Boultham. LN6 — 10 A4
Hall Dri, Canwick. LN4 — 11 E3
Hall Gdns. LN4 — 11 E3
Hall La. LN4 — 15 A3
Hallam Gro. LN6 — 10 A4
Halton Clo. LN6 — 8 A3
Hamilton Gro. LN6 — 16 C6
Hamilton Rd, North Hykeham. LN6 — 12 B4
Hamilton Rd, St Catherines. LN5 — 10 B4
Hampden Clo. LN6 — 16 B4
Hampden Way. LN5 — 17 C5
Hampton St. LN1 — 6 A5
Hannah Clo. LN4 — 15 C1
*Hannah Ho, Burwell Clo. LN2 — 7 E1
Harby Clo. LN6 — 13 F3
Hardwick Pl. LN2 — 6 D1
Harewood Av. LN6 — 13 E3
Harlaxton Clo. LN6 — 8 B5
Harlaxton Dri. LN6 — 8 C5
Harmston Clo. LN2 — 6 D1
Harpswell Rd. LN2 — 6 D3
Harrington Av. LN6 — 9 H4
Harrington Sq. LN4 — 14 E4
Harris Rd, Boultham Moor. LN6 — 9 G5
Harris Rd, Waddington. LN5 — 17 C4
Harrison Pl, Lincoln. LN1 — 6 C4
Harrison Pl, North Hykeham. LN6 — 12 B1
Harrow Clo. LN4 — 14 C2
Hartland Av. LN6 — 13 E5
Hartley St. LN2 — 7 F6
Hartsholme Dri. LN6 — 9 E4
Harvard Clo. LN4 — 14 D2
Harvey St. LN1 — 6 A6
Harwich Clo. LN5 — 13 H3
Hatcliffe Gdns. LN2 — 6 D2
Hathersage Av. LN6 — 12 C4
Hatton Clo. LN6 — 9 F4
Hawkshead Gro. LN2 — 6 D1
Hawksmoor Clo. LN6 — 12 C5
Hawthorn Av. LN3 — 13 G5
Hawthorn Chase. LN2 — 7 H3
Hawthorn Clo, Bracebridge Heath. LN4 — 15 C6
Hawthorn Clo, Heighington. LN4 — 14 E3
Hawthorn Rd, Cherry Willingham. LN3 — 4 A4
Hawthorn Rd, Lincoln. LN2 — 7 H3
Haydor Av. LN2 — 7 E2
Haze La. LN6 — 12 B5
Hazelwood Av. LN6 — 8 C3
Heath Rd, Bracebridge Heath. LN4 — 15 B6
Heath Rd, Nettleham. LN2 — 16 C1
Heathfield Av. LN4 — 15 D2
Hebden Moor Way. LN6 — 12 B5
Heighington Rd. LN4 — 11 E4
Helsby Rd. LN5 — 13 H2
Hemswell Av. LN6 — 9 E5
Henley St. LN5 — 10 B3
Henlow Clo. LN6 — 8 A4
Henry St. LN5 — 10 C3
Hereward St. LN1 — 6 C4
Hermit St. LN5 — 10 C2
Heron Vw. LN6 — 8 D3
Heron Walk. LN6 — 12 A5
Herrington Av. LN2 — 16 C1
Hewson Rd. LN1 — 6 A5
Heysham Clo. LN5 — 13 H3
Hibaldstow Clo. LN6 — 8 C5
Hibaldstow Rd. LN6 — 8 C4

Hickory Rd. LN6 — 8 C
Higgins Clo. LN6 — 8 D
High Dike. LN5 — 17 C
High Leas. LN2 — 16 D
High Meadow. LN4 — 14 C
High St, Branston. LN4 — 15 C
High St, Cherry Willingham. LN3 — 4 B
High St, Heighington. LN4 — 14 D
High St, Lincoln. LN5 — 5 B
High St, Nettleham. LN2 — 16 B
High St, New Boultham. LN5 — 10 B
High St, Reepham. LN3 — 4 C
High St, Skellingthorpe. LN6 — 16 B
High St, Waddington. LN5 — 17 B
High St, Washingborough. LN4 — 14 B
Highfield Av. LN6 — 9 G
Highfield Ter. LN6 — 13 E
Highfields. LN2 — 16 C
Higson Rd. LN1 — 6 A
Hill Top. LN5 — 17 B
Hillcroft. LN4 — 14 A
Hillman Clo. LN4 — 15 B
Hillside App. LN2 — 7 F
Hillside Av. LN2 — 7 F
Hobart Clo. LN5 — 13 G
Hodson Clo. LN6 — 16 C
Holdenby Clo. LN2 — 7 H
Holdenby Rd. LN2 — 7 H
Holly Clo. LN3 — 4 B
Holly Ct. LN5 — 13 H
Holly St. LN5 — 13 H
Hollywell Rd. LN5 — 13 G
Holmes Rd. LN1 — 6 B
Home Clo. LN4 — 15 B
Honington App. LN1 — 6 B
Honington Cres. LN1 — 6 A
Hood St. LN5 — 10 C
Hope St. LN5 — 10 D
Horner Clo. LN5 — 13 G
Horton St. LN2 — 7 E
Hout Clo. LN6 — 12 D
Howard St. LN1 — 6 A
Hudsons La. LN4 — 14 E
Hungate. LN1 — 5 B
Hunt Lea Av. LN6 — 9 G
Hunters Clo. LN5 — 17 C
Hurn Clo. LN6 — 8 A
Hurstwood Clo. LN2 — 7 F
Hutson Dri. LN6 — 12 D
Hyde Park Clo. LN6 — 13 E
Hykeham Rd. LN6 — 13 F

Icknield Clo. LN4 — 15 C

INDUSTRIAL & RETAIL:
Allenby Road Ind Est. LN3 — 7 G
Great Northern Ind Est. LN5 — 11 E
Lincoln Ind Park. LN6 — 8 B
Newport Business Pk. LN2 — 7 F
Outercircle Ind Est. LN2 — 7 F
Sunningdale Trading Est. LN6 — 10 A
The Quarry Ind Est. LN5 — 17 C
Westminster Ind Est. LN6 — 12 B
Ingham Clo. LN6 — 13 F
Ingleby Cres. LN2 — 6 C
Inns Clo. LN6 — 12 D
Ironstone Clo. LN2 — 7 F

Jacobean Rd. LN6 — 8 C
Jaguar Dri. LN6 — 12 B
James St. LN2 — 5 C
Jarvis Clo. LN6 — 9 E
*Jarvis Ho, Jarvis Clo. LN6 — 9 E
Jasmin Rd. LN6 — 8 B
Jason Rd. LN6 — 13 E
Jellicoe Av. LN2 — 7 G
Jenson Rd. LN4 — 15 B
Jermyn Mews. LN4 — 14 D

usalem Rd. LN6 16 A6
esmond Vw,
Edendale Gdns. LN1 6 B1
ssop Clo. LN3 4 B5
hn St. LN2 5 E3
hnson Dri. LN4 15 B5
hnson Villas. LN4 15 D1
bilee Clo,
Cherry Willingham. LN3 4 B4
bilee Clo,
North Hykeham. LN6 12 D5
lia Rd. LN4 14 D3
niper Clo, Bracebridge
Low Fields. LN5 13 G4
niper Clo, Branston. LN4 15 C2

adby Clo. LN6 9 E5
ats Clo. LN2 7 F2
ddington Av. LN1 6 C1
eble Dri. LN4 14 D2
lls Clo. LN5 13 H3
lsey St. LN1 5 B3
lstern Clo. LN6 8 B5
lstern Rd. LN6 8 B5
mble Clo. LN6 8 B4
ndall Clo. LN2 17 B2
nilworth Dri. LN6 9 H6
nnedy Rd. LN4 15 B5
nnel La. LN3 4 A1
nner Clo. LN6 9 F6
nneth St. LN1 6 C3
nt St. LN2 7 F6
nyon Clo. LN4 14 D4
rrison View. LN2 16 D1
ershaw Vw,
Riverton Clo. LN1 6 B1
steven Ct. LN6 12 B4
steven St. LN5 10 C1
strel Clo. LN6 8 D3
xby Mill Clo. LN6 12 C6
burn Cres. LN6 9 F5
nder Av. LN6 13 E4
ng Dri. LN4 15 C6
ng St. LN5 10 C2
ngfisher Clo. LN6 8 C3
ngsdown Rd. LN6 8 B4
ngsley Rd. LN6 8 A6
ngsley St. LN1 6 B4
ngsway,
Lincoln. LN5 10 D3
ngsway,
Nettleham. LN2 16 B2
nloss Clo. LN6 8 B5
pling Clo. LN2 7 E2
rkby St. LN5 10 C2
rmington Clo. LN6 8 B5
ight Pl. LN5 10 C3
ight St. LN5 10 C3

burnum Clo,
Branston. LN4 15 C2
burnum Clo,
North Hykeham. LN6 13 E3
burnum Ct. LN3 4 D2
burnum Dri. LN3 4 A6
ceby St. LN2 7 E6
cy Clo. LN2 16 D3
dds Mill Clo. LN6 12 C6
dy Bower Clo. LN6 13 E4
dymeers Rd. LN3 4 B5
gonda Clo. LN4 15 B6
ke View Clo. LN6 12 B5
ke View Rd. LN6 9 H6
mb Gdns. LN2 7 E3
ncaster Clo. LN5 17 C5
ncaster Pl. LN5 10 C2
ncaster Way. LN6 16 B4
ncewood Gdns. LN6 8 C3
ncia Cres. LN4 15 B6
ndmere Gro. LN6 8 D2
ney Clo. LN2 7 F2
ngley Rd. LN6 12 B4
ngor Clo. LN6 8 A5
ngton Clo. LN2 7 E2
ngworth Gate. LN2 5 D1
nnimore Clo. LN5 13 H2
nsdowne Av. LN6 9 H6

Lapwing Clo. LN6 16 C5
Larch Av. LN2 16 D2
Larchwood Cres. LN6 8 B3
Larkin Av. LN3 4 A6
Larkspur Rd. LN2 7 G2
Larne Clo. LN5 13 G4
Larne Rd. LN5 13 H3
Laughton Cres. LN2 7 E2
Laughton Way. LN2 6 C1
Laughton Way Nth. LN2 6 C1
Laurel Clo. LN5 13 H1
Lavender Clo. LN5 13 G4
Lavenham Gro. LN6 13 E1
Lawn Ct. LN1 5 B1
Lawrence Clo. LN6 9 G5
*Lechler Clo,
Cotton Smith Way. LN2 16 C1
Leconfield Clo. LN6 8 B5
Leconfield Rd. LN6 8 B5
Lee Av. LN4 14 D2
Lee Rd. LN2 6 D4
Leeming Clo. LN6 8 C6
Legbourne Clo. LN1 6 B2
Leicester Clo. LN4 14 C2
Leighton Cres. LN6 9 F5
Lenton Grn. LN2 7 E2
Leonards La. LN2 5 D1
Lewis St. LN5 10 C2
Leyburn Rd. LN6 12 D2
Lichfield Rd. LN4 15 C4
Lilac Clo. LN6 8 B3
Lilford Clo. LN2 7 H2
Lilford Rd. LN2 7 G2
Lillicrap Ct. LN1 5 B1
Lilys Rd. LN1 6 C4
Lime Cres. LN5 13 G5
Lime Gro. LN3 4 A5
Lime Kiln Way. LN2 7 F5
Lime Tree Clo. LN2 8 D4
Limelands, Lincoln. LN2 5 E1
*Limelands, All Saints La,
Nettleham. LN2 16 B2
Lincoln Av. LN6 10 A4
Lincoln By-Pass,
Birchwood. LN6 8 A5
Lincoln By-Pass,
Lincoln. LN2 6 A1
Lincoln Dri. LN5 17 C5
Lincoln Rd,
Branston. LN4 15 A1
Lincoln Rd,
Canwick. LN4 11 E4
Lincoln Rd,
Cherry Willingham. LN3 4 C6
Lincoln Rd,
Nettleham. LN2 16 A3
Lincoln Rd,
North Hykeham. LN6 13 E4
Lincoln Rd,
Skellingthorpe. LN6 16 C4
Lincoln Rd,
Washingborough. LN4 14 A1
Linden Av. LN4 15 B1
*Linden Ct,
Beech Clo. LN4 15 B6
Lindholme Rd. LN6 8 C6
Lindrick Clo. LN4 14 D3
Lindum Av. LN2 5 D2
Lindum Rd. LN2 5 C3
Lindum Ter. LN2 5 D2
Linnet Clo. LN6 8 C3
Lintin Clo. LN4 14 D4
Linton St. LN5 10 D2
Lisburn Clo. LN5 13 H4
Lissett Clo. LN6 8 A5
Lissington Clo. LN2 6 C2
Little Bargate St. LN5 10 C3
Liverpool Dri. LN6 16 C6
Locking Clo. LN6 8 C6
Lodge Dri. LN4 15 D2
Lodge La. LN2 16 D2
London Rd. LN4 15 B4
Long Leys Rd. LN1 6 A4
Longdales Rd. LN2 6 C3
Longland Walk. LN2 7 G2
Lonsdale Ct. LN4 14 B2
Lonsdale Pl. LN5 10 C2

Lorne St. LN5 10 D1
Lotus Clo. LN5 17 C5
Low Moor Rd. LN6 12 C1
Low Park La. LN3 14 F3
Lower Church Rd. LN6 16 C4
Lower High St. LN5 17 B5
Lucy Tower St. LN1 5 A3
Ludford Dri. LN6 9 F5
Lumley Pl. LN5 10 C2
Lupin Rd. LN2 7 F2
Lurgan Clo. LN5 13 H3
Luton Clo. LN6 8 B3
Lydd Clo. LN6 8 B5
Lyneham Clo. LN6 8 B4
Lynmouth Clo. LN6 13 E4
Lytham Clo. LN4 14 D2
Lytton St. LN2 5 E4

Macaulay Dri. LN2 7 E3
McInnes St. LN2 7 F6
Macmillan Av. LN6 12 B5
Magnolia Clo. LN4 15 C1
Magpie Clo. LN6 16 B5
Main Av. LN4 15 B5
Main Rd. LN4 14 B1
Mainwaring Rd. LN2 6 D4
Malham Clo. LN6 8 C2
Malham Dri. LN6 8 C1
Mallard Clo. LN6 16 B6
Mallard Ct. LN6 12 A5
Mallard Gro. LN6 8 D3
Malt Kiln La. LN5 17 B6
Malton Rd. LN6 12 D3
Malus Clo. LN4 15 C2
Malvern Av. LN4 14 D2
Malvern Clo, Bracebridge
Low Fields. LN5 13 H2
Malvern Clo,
North Hykeham. LN6 12 C6
Manby St. LN5 10 B5
Manchester Rd. LN5 17 C6
Manor Clo. LN2 6 D4
Manor Ct,
Nettleham. LN2 16 B2
Manor Ct,
Sudbrooke. LN2 17 A1
Manor Dri. LN2 17 B2
Manor Dri, Reepham. LN3 4 C3
Manor La. LN2 17 B6
Manor Leas Clo. LN6 13 F3
Manor Rd, Lincoln. LN2 6 D4
Manor Rd,
North Hykeham. LN6 12 D5
Manor Rd,
Washingborough. LN4 14 B2
Manse Av. LN5 13 H1
Mansford Clo. LN2 16 C1
Manton Rd. LN2 6 C3
Maple Clo,
Bracebridge Heath. LN4 15 C6
Maple Clo, Bracebridge
Low Fields. LN5 13 G6
Maple Dri. LN5 17 B2
Maple St. LN5 10 B6
Mareham Clo. LN4 15 C6
Marham Clo. LN6 8 B3
Marigold Clo. LN2 7 F1
Marina Clo. LN5 17 C5
Marjorie Av. LN6 10 A3
Marjorie Ct. LN6 10 A3
Marlborough Av. LN4 14 C2
Marlborough Clo. LN2 7 F1
Marlborough Ct. LN4 14 B2
Marlowe Dri. LN2 7 E3
Marne Gdns. LN1 6 B3
Martin Clo,
Heighington. LN4 14 D4
Martin Clo,
Skellingthorpe. LN6 16 B6
Martin St. LN5 10 C2
Massey Rd. LN2 6 D4
Matilda Rd. LN6 10 A2
Matlock Dri. LN6 12 D4
Maxwell Av. LN6 9 G3
May Cres. LN1 6 B5
Mayall Ct. LN5 17 B6
Mayfair Av. LN6 10 A4

Mead Clo. LN6 13 E1
Mead Way. LN3 4 C5
Meadow Clo,
North Hykeham. LN6 12 D6
Meadow Clo,
Reepham. LN3 4 D2
Meadow Lake. LN6 8 C3
Meadow La. LN6 12 D6
Meadow Way. LN4 15 C6
Meadows La. LN3 4 D2
Medway Cres. LN6 13 F4
Melbourne Clo. LN6 8 C4
Melbourne Rd. LN6 8 C4
Melbourne Way. LN5 13 G6
Mellows Clo. LN3 4 C2
Melville Clo. LN4 15 C3
Melville St. LN5 5 C4
Mendip Av. LN6 12 C6
Mendip Clo. LN5 13 H2
Mere Rd, Branston. LN4 15 C3
Mere Rd,
Waddington. LN5 17 C6
Merrycock La. LN4 14 D4
Metheringham Clo. LN6 8 C4
Meynell Av. LN6 9 H4
Michaelgate. LN1 5 B2
Middle St, Burton. LN1 6 A1
Middle St,
North Hykeham. LN6 12 D6
Middlebrook Clo. LN6 9 F6
Middlebrook Rd. LN6 9 F6
Middletons Field. LN2 6 C4
Midholm. LN3 4 B5
Midville Clo. LN1 6 C2
Midway.Clo LN2 16 D2
Mildenhall Dri. LN6 8 A3
Mildway St. LN1 6 C4
Mill Hill. LN2 16 C2
Mill La, Boultham. LN5 10 B2
Mill La,
Heighington. LN4 14 D3
Mill La,
North Hykeham. LN6 12 C6
Mill Mere Rd. LN5 17 B5
Mill Moor Way. LN6 12 B5
Mill Rd. LN1 5 A1
Mill Row. LN1 6 B4
Mill Stone La. LN5 17 B5
Millbeck Dri. LN2 6 D1
Millbrook Clo. LN6 12 C5
Millers Clo. LN4 14 D3
Millers Dale. LN6 12 D4
Millstream Rd. LN4 14 D3
Milman Rd. LN2 5 F3
Milton Clo. LN4 15 A1
Milton St. LN5 10 B5
Minster Ct. LN4 15 B4
Minster Dri. LN3 4 B4
Minster Yard. LN2 5 C2
Mint La. LN1 5 B3
Mint St. LN1 5 B3
Minting Clo. LN1 6 C2
Mitchell Clo. LN6 16 B5
Monks Ley Ter. LN2 5 E2
Monks Manor Ct. LN2 5 F1
Monks Manor Dri. LN2 5 F1
Monks Rd. LN2 5 C3
Monks Way. LN2 7 F6
Mons Rd. LN1 6 B3
Monsale Dale. LN6 12 D4
Monson Park. LN6 16 B5
Monson St. LN5 10 C2
Montague Rd. LN4 11 E3
Montague St. LN2 5 D3
Montague Ter. LN2 5 D3
Montaigne Clo. LN2 7 G2
Montaigne Cres. LN2 7 G2
Montaigne Gdn. LN2 7 G2
Montrose Clo. LN6 12 C5
Moor La,
Branston. LN4 15 D3
Moor La,
North Hykeham. LN6 12 C4
Moor La,
Reepham. LN3 4 D2
Moor St. LN1 6 A5
Moorby Clo. LN1 6 C2

Name	Ref
Moorland Av. LN6	9 F6
Moorland Clo. LN6	9 E6
Moorland Cres. LN6	9 G5
Moorland Way. LN6	9 E6
Morton Dri. LN6	9 E5
Motherby Hill. LN1	5 B2
Motherby La. LN1	5 B3
Mount Rd. LN4	15 B5
Mount St. LN1	6 B4
Mountbatten Ct. LN4	14 B2
Mourn Ter. LN5	13 H3
Moxons La. LN5	17 B5
Much La. LN1	5 B3
Mulberry Av. LN6	13 E4
Mulberry Clo. LN5	13 G5
Murdock Rd. LN5	10 B5
Naam Gro. LN1	6 B4
Naam Pl. LN1	6 B4
Napier St. LN2	5 E3
*Natal Vw, Allandale Clo. LN1	6 B1
Neale Rd. LN6	12 C6
Neile Clo. LN2	7 G3
Nelson Dri. LN4	14 B2
Nelson St. LN1	6 A6
Nelthorpe St. LN5	10 C2
Nene Park. LN6	12 B5
Nene Rd. LN1	6 B1
Nettleham Clo. LN2	6 D3
Nettleham Rd. LN2	5 D1
Nettleton Clo. LN4	15 C1
New Cres. LN3	4 B5
Newark Rd, Bracebridge. LN5	10 A6
Newark Rd, North Hykeham. LN6	12 A6
Newcot La. LN4	14 F4
Newhaven Dri. LN5	13 H3
Newland. LN1	5 A3
Newland St West. LN1	5 A2
Newport. LN1	6 C4
Newport Ct. LN1	5 C1
Newport Cres. LN5	17 C4
Newstead Av. LN3	4 B6
Newton St. LN2	5 C4
Nightingale Cres. LN6	8 C3
Nocton Dri. LN2	6 C1
Norfolk Cres. LN4	15 B4
Norfolk St. LN1	6 A5
Norman St. LN5	5 C4
Norris St. LN5	10 C2
North Ct. LN2	16 C2
North La. LN3	4 B2
North Par. LN1	5 A2
North St. LN2	16 C2
Northfield Av. LN2	17 B1
Northgate. LN2	5 C1
Northorpe Clo. LN6	9 E5
Norwich Clo. LN4	14 E2
Norwich Dri. LN4	15 C4
Nottingham Ter. LN2	5 D2
Nursery Gro. LN2	6 D3
Nurses La. LN6	16 B4
Oak Clo. LN2	17 B3
Oak Cres. LN3	4 A6
Oak Hill. LN4	14 B1
Oakdene Av. LN4	15 C4
Oakfield St. LN2	5 F3
Oakland Clo. LN1	6 B2
Oakwood Av. LN6	8 C3
Oakwood Clo. LN3	4 B5
Occupation Rd. LN1	5 B1
Ockbrook Ct. LN1	6 C4
Old Chapel Rd. LN6	16 B4
Old Oak Rise. LN6	16 C5
Old Pond Clo. LN6	8 C3
Old Stackyard. LN4	14 E3
Olive St. LN1	6 B4
Orchard Garth. LN5	17 A4
Orchard Clo. LN3	4 A5
Orchard St. LN1	5 A3
Orchard Way. LN2	16 C1
Orchid Rd. LN5	13 G4
Osborne Clo. LN1	6 C3
Oulton Clo. LN6	13 E4
Oundle Clo. LN4	14 C2
Outer Circle Dri. LN2	7 E2
Outer Circle Grn. LN2	7 F3
Outer Circle Rd. LN2	7 F3
Oval App. LN2	7 E2
Oxen Park Clo. LN2	6 D1
Oxford Clo. LN4	14 C3
Oxford St. LN5	5 C4
Paddock Clo. LN4	15 B6
Paddock La. LN4	15 C2
Park Av, Hartsholme. LN6	9 E4
Park Av, Washingborough. LN4	14 C2
Park Clo. LN2	17 C2
Park Cres. LN4	14 C2
Park La, Bracebridge Heath. LN4	15 B4
Park La, Heighington. LN4	14 E3
Park La, Washingborough. LN4	14 C2
Park St. LN1	5 B3
Park View Av. LN4	15 B2
Parker Av. LN5	13 H2
Parker Cres. LN5	13 H2
Parkhill. LN3	4 B5
Parksgate Av. LN6	12 D1
Parkside. LN2	16 C2
Pateley Moor Clo. LN6	12 C6
Peak Dale. LN6	12 C4
Pear Tree Clo. LN6	8 C3
Peddars Ct. LN4	15 C6
Peel St. LN5	10 B3
Pelham La. LN4	11 E3
Pelham St. LN2	5 C4
Pendine Cres. LN6	13 E5
Penfold La. LN4	14 C1
Pennell St. LN5	10 B2
Pennycress Cres. LN2	7 F2
Penrose Clo. LN6	12 D6
Pentland Dri. LN6	12 C6
Peppercorn Clo. LN6	10 B2
Percy St. LN2	5 F3
Perney Cres. LN6	12 C6
Pershore Way. LN6	8 B5
Pewlham Clo. LN2	17 B2
Phillip Ct. LN6	12 D5
Photinia Clo. LN4	15 C1
Pietermaritz St. LN1	6 B1
*Pietermaritz Vw, Pietermaritz St. LN1	6 B1
Pinder Clo. LN4	14 A2
Pine Clo, Lincoln. LN1	6 C1
Pine Clo, Waddington. LN5	13 G6
Pine Way. LN4	15 B1
Pioneer Way. LN6	12 C1
Pitts Rd. LN4	14 C2
Plough La. LN3	4 D2
Plover Gro. LN6	8 D3
Poachers La. LN2	17 B1
Poachers Mdw. LN2	16 D2
Poplar St. LN5	10 B6
Portland St. LN5	10 C2
Pottergate. LN2	5 D2
Pottergate Clo. LN5	17 C4
Potterhanworth Rd. LN4	14 E4
Prenton Clo. LN6	13 E1
Prestwick Clo. LN6	8 B3
Prial Av. LN6	9 G5
Prial Clo. LN6	9 G5
Primrose Clo. LN5	13 G4
Princess Royal Clo. LN2	5 E2
Princess St. LN5	10 B2
Prior St. LN5	10 C2
Proctors Rd. LN2	7 F4
Pullan Clo. LN5	13 H3
Pyke Rd. LN6	12 B1
Queen Cres. LN1	6 B5
Queen Elizabeth Rd. LN1	6 A2
Queen Mary Rd. LN1	6 A2
Queen St. LN5	10 B3
Queensbury Ct. LN4	14 B2
Queensway, Lincoln. LN2	5 E1
Queensway, Skellingthorpe. LN6	16 B6
Quintin Clo. LN4	15 B5
Quorn Dri. LN6	9 H4
Railway Pk Clo. LN6	10 A2
Railway Pk Mews. LN6	10 A2
Rasen La. LN1	6 B4
Rauceby Ter. LN1	5 B2
Ravendale Dri. LN2	6 D2
Ravensmoor Clo. LN6	12 C5
Raynor Clo. LN4	14 A2
Reading Clo. LN4	14 E2
Rectory La, Branston. LN4	15 C3
Rectory La, Waddington. LN5	17 B6
Redbourne Dri. LN2	6 D1
Redcar Clo. LN6	12 D2
Redcote Dri. LN6	12 D1
Redhall Dri. LN4	15 B4
Redhall La. LN4	15 B4
Redwing Clo. LN6	16 B5
Redwing Gro. LN6	8 D3
Redwood Dri. LN5	13 G6
Regent Av. LN6	8 B2
Regents Park Clo. LN6	12 D5
Reid Ct. LN4	15 C1
Remigius Gro. LN2	7 F3
Renault Ter. LN4	15 B6
Renerew Clo. LN5	13 G4
Renerew Rd. LN5	13 G4
Reption Clo. LN4	14 D2
Reservoir St. LN1	5 B1
Retief Clo. LN1	6 A1
*Retief Vw, Retief Clo. LN1	6 A1
Revesby Clo. LN6	9 E5
Revesby Sq. LN4	14 E4
Reynolds Dri. LN6	9 G5
Richards Av. LN6	12 D2
Richmond Dri. LN6	12 D3
*Richmond Gro, Richmond Rd. LN1	6 A5
Richmond Rd. LN1	6 A5
*Ridge Vw, Retief Clo. LN1	6 A1
Ridge Way. LN4	15 C5
Ridgeview Rd. LN4	15 A5
Ridgeway. LN2	16 D2
Ridgewell Clo. LN6	8 C4
Rigsmoor Clo. LN6	12 C6
Riley Clo. LN4	15 B6
Ringwood Clo. LN6	8 C2
Ripley Dri. LN6	13 E3
Ripon St. LN5	10 C2
Risby Grn. LN6	9 E4
Riseholme La. LN2	16 A2
Riseholme Rd. LN1	6 C1
Riverdale. LN2	16 D2
Rivermead. LN6	13 G2
Rivermead Clo. LN6	13 G2
Riverton Clo. LN1	6 B1
*Riverton Vw, Riverton Clo. LN1	6 B1
Robert Tressell Wk. LN2	7 F2
Robertson Clo. LN5	17 B5
Robertson Rd. LN5	12 D5
Robey St. LN5	10 B3
Rochester Dri. LN6	8 C1
Rolleston Dri. LN2	6 C2
Roman Pavement. LN2	7 F5
Roman Wharf. LN1	6 A6
Romney Clo. LN6	9 G5
Romney Dri. LN6	13 F1
Rookery La. LN6	9 H5
Rope Walk. LN6	5 A4
Rosebery Av. LN1	6 A5
Rosedale Clo. LN6	13 E3
Rosemary La. LN2	5 D3
Roseum Clo. LN6	12 C1
Rosewood Clo. LN6	8 B3
Rothwell Rd. LN2	6 C3
Roughton Ct. LN2	6 D1
Rowan Ct. LN4	14 D3
Rowan Rd, North Hykeham. LN6	12 D3
Rowan Rd, Waddington. LN5	13 C
Roxborough Clo. LN6	8 D
Roxby Clo. LN6	9
Royal Oak La. LN4	14 C
Roydon Gro. LN6	9 C
Ruckland Av. LN1	6 C
Rudgard Av. LN3	4 B
Rudgard La. LN1	5 A
Rufford Grn. LN1	9 H
Runswick Clo. LN6	13 E
Ruskin Av. LN2	7 E
Ruskin Grn. LN2	7 E
Rusland Clo. LN2	6 D
Russell Av. LN6	12 D
Russell St. LN1	5 E
Russell St. LN5	10 E
Rydal Clo. LN6	8 C
Ryecroft. LN5	13 H
Sadler Rd. LN6	8 A
St Aidens Rd. LN6	12 C
St Albans Clo. LN6	15 C
St Andrews Dri. LN6	10 A
St Andrews Gdns. LN6	9 H
St Andrews Pl. LN5	10 C
St Andrews St. LN5	10 C
St Annes Clo. LN2	5 F
St Annes Rd. LN2	5 F
St Aubins Cres. LN4	14 E
St Benedicts Clo. LN6	12 C
St Benedicts Sq. LN5	5 E
*St Botolphs Ct, St Botolphs Cres. LN5	10 B
St Botolphs Cres. LN5	10 B
St Catherines. LN5	10 B
St Catherines Ct. LN5	10 B
St Catherines Gro. LN5	10 B
St Catherines Rd. LN5	10 B
St Claires Ct. LN6	8 C
St Clements Ct. LN1	5 C
St Clements Rd. LN6	12 C
St Crispins Clo. LN6	12 C
St Davids Clo. LN3	4 B
St Davids Rd. LN6	12 B
St Edwards Dri. LN2	17 B
St Faiths St. LN1	5 A
St Francis Clo. LN6	12 C
St Georges Clo. LN6	12 C
St Giles Av. LN2	5 D
St Helens Av. LN6	9 G
St Hilarys Clo. LN6	12 B
St Hugh St. LN2	5 D
St Hughs Clo. LN3	4 C
St Hughs Dri. LN6	12 C
St Johns Av, Cherry Willingham. LN3	4 B
St Johns Av, North Hykeham. LN6	12 C
St Johns La. LN6	12 C
St Johns Rd, Bracebridge Heath. LN4	15 B
St Johns Rd, Lincoln. LN1	6 C
St Johns Sq. LN6	15 B
St Lukes Clo. LN3	4 C
St Margarets Clo. LN6	13 F
St Margarets Gdns. LN6	13 F
St Mark St. LN5	5 B
St Marks Av. LN3	4 C
St Martins La. LN2	5 B
St Martins St. LN2	5 C
St Marys Rd. LN6	12 C
St Marys St. LN5	5 B
St Matthews Clo, Boultham. LN6	10 A
St Matthews Clo, Cherry Willingham. LN3	4 B
St Michaels Clo. LN5	17 B
St Nicholas St. LN1	6 C
St Pauls Av. LN3	4 B
St Pauls La. LN1	6 C
St Peters Av, Boultham Moor. LN6	9 H
St Peters Av, Cherry Willingham. LN3	4 B
St Peters Av, North Hykeham. LN6	12 C

Street	Ref		Street	Ref
Rumbolds St. LN2	5 C3		Somersby Clo. LN6	13 G1
Simons Dri. LN3	4 B4		Somerton Gate La. LN5	17 A6
Swithins Sq. LN2	5 C3		Somerville St. LN5	17 A4
lisbury Dri. LN4	15 C4		Somerville Ct. LN5	17 A4
lix App. LN6	8 B3		Sorrel Ct. LN6	8 B3
ttergate. LN2	5 C3		South Par. LN1	6 B5
lters Clo. LN4	15 C6		South Park. LN5	10 B4
nders Clo. LN1	6 A1		South Park Av. LN5	10 C3
anders Vw,			Southdown. LN5	13 H4
Sanders Clo. LN1	6 A1		Southland Dri. LN6	13 F2
ndra Cres. LN4	14 D3		Southwell Ct. LN4	15 C4
ndtoft Clo. LN6	8 C5		Spa Buildings. LN2	5 D3
ndwell Dri. LN6	8 C2		Spa Rd. LN2	5 E4
nsford Grn. LN6	9 F6		Spa St. LN2	7 E6
tinwood Clo. LN6	8 C3		Spanby Dri. N6	9 F4
usthorpe St. LN5	10 C3		Sparrow La. LN2	5 D3
ville St. LN5	10 B5		Spencer St. LN5	10 B3
rkly Rd. LN1	16 B4		Spennymoor Clo. LN6	12 B5
xon St. LN1	6 C4		Sperrin Clo. LN5	13 H3
ampton Av. LN6	9 E5		Spilsby Clo. LN6	8 C4
arle Clo. LN6	13 E3		Spirea App. LN6	8 B3
awby Cres. LN6	9 E4		Spital St. LN1	6 C4
nool La,			Spring Hill, Lincoln. LN1	5 B2
Canwick. LN4	11 E4		Spring Hill, Reepham. LN3	4 C2
nool La,			Springfield Clo,	
North Hykeham. LN6	12 D5		Branston. LN4	15 C3
nool La,			Springfield Clo,	
Washingborough. LN4	14 C1		Lincoln. LN1	6 C4
opwick Pl. LN2	6 C1		Spruce Cres. LN4	15 B1
orer St. LN5	10 C2		Squires Pl. LN2	16 D2
othern La. LN2	17 B2		Staffordshire Cres. LN6	8 D4
othern Rd. LN2	16 C1		Stainton Gdns. LN1	6 B2
ott Gdns. LN2	7 F3		Stamp End. LN2	5 E4
otton Dri. LN6	9 F5		Stane Dri. LN4	15 C6
arby Rd. LN2	7 E1		Stanley Cres. LN4	15 B4
dgebrook Clo. LN2	6 C1		Stanley Pl. LN5	10 C2
dgemoor Clo. LN6	12 C5		Stanley St. LN5	10 B5
ely Ct. LN4	14 D3		Stapleford Av. LN2	6 C2
lby Clo. LN6	13 E3		Staples La. LN5	17 B2
vern St. LN1	6 A6		Station Field. LN6	16 C5
well Rd. LN2	5 E1		Station Rd,	
wells Walk. LN5	10 B		Branston. LN4	15 D2
wstern Clo. LN4	15 C6		Station Rd,	
aftesbury Av. LN6	8 C1		Heighington. LN4	14 D4
akespeare St. LN5	10 B3		Station Rd,	
eepwash La. LN4	14 C3		North Hykeham. LN6	12 B2
elley Dri. LN2	7 E3		Station Rd,	
epherds Way. LN2	17 B1		Reepham. LN3	4 D2
heppard Ct,			Station Rd,	
Western Av. LN4	15 B5		Waddington. LN5	17 A4
eppards Clo. LN4	14 D3		Staunton St. LN1	6 A6
eraton Clo. LN6	8 C5		Staverton Rd. LN6	8 A3
erbrooke St. LN2	7 G6		Steep Hill. LN2	5 C2
eridan Clo. LN2	7 F2		Steeping Ct. LN1	6 B1
erwood Dri. LN5	13 H5		Stenigot Clo. LN6	8 C5
othorpe Dri. LN2	17 B2		Stenigot Gro. LN6	8 C5
othorpe Gdns. LN5	11 E4		Stenigot Rd. LN6	8 C5
othorpe St. LN5	10 C2		Stevenson Clo. LN4	14 D4
llaw Gro. LN5	13 G3		Stewards Way. LN4	15 B5
lney St. LN5	13 G3		Stirling Way. LN6	16 B5
ver St, Branston. LN4	15 C3		Stone La. LN5	17 B5
ver St, Lincoln. LN2	5 B3		Stone Moor Rd. LN6	12 C6
nons Grn. LN6	9 H6		Stonefield Av. LN2	6 C4
cil Bank. LN5	10 C3		Stonelea Clo. LN4	15 D2
cil St. LN5	5 C4		Stoney Yd. LN6	16 B4
fields Clo. LN6	9 F5		Stoyles Way. LN4	14 D3
ellingthorpe Rd. LN6	8 C1		Strahane Clo. LN5	13 G3
erries Clo. LN6	13 E5		Strait. LN2	5 C2
aford Rd,			Strubby Clo. LN6	8 C4
Bracebridge Heath. LN4	15 B5		Sturgate Clo. LN6	8 B5
aford Rd,			Sturton Clo. LN2	6 D2
Branston. LN4	15 D3		Sudbrooke Dri. LN2	6 D2
essor St. LN5	17 C4		Sudbrooke Holme Dri. LN2	17 B2
iths St. LN5	10 B3		Sudbrooke La,	
nooting La. LN3	4 D2		Nettleham. LN2	16 D2
aith Clo. LN6	8 B5		Sudbrooke La,	
etterton Clo. LN6	8 B4		Sudbrooke. LN2	17 A2
owberry Gdns. LN6	8 B3		Sudbury Clo. LN6	13 E1
owdon Clo. LN5	13 H2		Sunbeam Av. LN6	12 B5
			Sunderland Clo. LN6	16 B5
			Sunfield Cres. LN6	8 C2
			Sunningdale Dri. LN6	10 A3
			Sunningdale Gro. LN4	12 D2
			Sutton Clo,	
			Nettleham. LN2	16 B2
			Sutton Clo,	
			Washingborough. LN4	14 A2

Street	Ref		Street	Ref
Swaby Clo. LN2	6 B1		Thorngate. LN2	5 C3
Swallow Av. LN6	16 B5		Thornton Clo,	
Swallowbeck Av. LN6	13 E2		Hartsholme. LN6	9 F4
Swan St. LN2	5 C3		Thornton Clo,	
Swanholme Clo. LN6	12 C1		Washingborough. LN4	14 A2
Swayne Clo. LN2	7 G2		Thornton Way. LN3	4 B5
Swaythling Clo. LN6	8 D6		Thorpe Av. LN1	6 A2
Swift Gdns. LN2	7 E2		Thurlby Clo. LN4	14 A2
Swift Grn. LN2	7 E2		Thurlby Cres. LN2	7 E1
Sycamore Clo,			Thurlow Ct. LN2	7 G2
Birchwood. LN6	8 D4		Timms La. LN5	17 B6
Sycamore Clo,			Tinkers La. LN5	17 B6
Branston. LN4	15 C1		Tobruk Clo. LN1	6 B2
Sycamore Clo,			Toronto St. LN2	7 F6
Cherry Willingham. LN3	4 B6		Torrington Rd. LN2	6 C1
Sycamore Cres. LN6	8 D4		Tothill Clo. LN6	9 E4
Sycamore Dri. LN5	13 G6		Tower Av,	
Sycamore Gro. LN4	15 C6		Bracebridge Heath. LN4	15 B5
Sympson Clo. LN2	7 G3		Tower Av, Lincoln. LN2	7 G5
Syringa Grn. LN6	8 B3		Tower Cres. LN2	7 G5
Syston Gro. LN5	13 H2		Tower Dri. LN2	7 G5
Sywell Clo. LN6	8 B6		*Tower Flats,	
			Tower Gdns. LN2	7 G5
Tamar Way. LN6	13 E4		Tower Gdns. LN2	7 G5
Tanners La. LN5	10 B2		Toynton Clo. LN6	13 F2
Tealby St. LN5	10 B3		Trafalgar Ct. LN4	14 B1
Tedder Dri. LN5	17 C5		Trelawney Cres. LN1	6 B1
Teesdale Clo. LN6	8 B2		Trenchard Sq. LN4	17 C4
Tempest St. LN2	5 F3		*Trent Vw,	
Temple Gdns. LN2	5 C2		Welland Rd. LN1	6 A2
Tennyson St. LN1	6 A5		Trevose Dri. LN6	13 E5
Tentercroft St. LN5	10 C1		Tritton Rd,	
Tetney Clo. LN1	6 C1		Boultham Moor. LN6	9 E6
Thackers La. LN4	15 C3		Tritton Rd,	
The Avenue. LN1	5 A3		North Hykeham. LN6	12 D1
The Chalfonts. LN4	15 D1		Trollope St. LN5	10 C2
The Chestnuts. LN2	16 B2		Troon Clo. LN4	14 D2
The Close. LN2	15 C5		Troutbeck Clo. LN2	7 E1
The Cottage Paddock. LN5	13 F1		Truro Dri. LN6	8 A3
The Crescent,			*Tudor Ho,	
Bracebridge Heath. LN4	15 C5		Weldon Gdns. LN2	6 D1
The Crescent,			Tudor Rd. LN6	8 D5
Nettleham. LN2	16 C2		Tulip Wood Av. LN6	8 C3
The Croft. LN2	16 C2		Turnberry Clo. LN4	14 D3
The Dales,			Turnbury Clo. LN6	8 B4
Nettleham. LN2	16 C3		Turner Av. LN6	9 F5
The Dene. LN2	16 C1		Turner St. LN1	6 B4
The Dene,			Tyne Clo. LN6	13 E4
Skellingthorpe. LN6	16 C5			
The Forum. LN6	13 E3		Uffington Av. LN6	9 F5
The Green,			Uffington Clo. LN6	9 F4
Nettleham. LN2	16 C2		Uldale Clo. LN6	8 C2
The Green,			Ullswater Clo. LN6	13 E4
Reepham. LN3	4 D2		Union Rd. LN1	5 B2
The Grove. LN2	6 D4		Unity Sq. LN2	5 C3
The Hawthorns. LN2	16 D2		Upper Lindum St. LN2	5 D2
The Hill. LN6	16 B4		Upper Long Leys Rd. LN1	5 A1
The Leys. LN3	4 B5		Upper Saxon St. LN1	6 C4
The Link. LN4	15 B4		Urban St. LN5	10 B6
The Mall Shopping			Usher Av. LN6	9 G5
Centre. LN1	5 B3		Usher Grn. LN6	9 G5
The Mead. LN6	13 E1			
The Oaks. LN2	16 D2		Valentine Rd. LN6	10 A2
The Orchard. LN4	14 A1		Valiant St. LN5	17 C5
The Oval. LN2	7 E2		Valley Rd. LN5	13 G5
The Paddock,			Vanwall Dri. LN5	17 C5
Canwick. LN4	11 E4		Vauxhall Rd. LN4	15 B6
The Paddock,			Verdon Clo. LN1	6 B2
Cherry Willingham. LN3	4 B5		Vere St. LN1	6 C4
The Paddock,			Vernon St. LN5	10 B2
Skellingthorpe. LN6	16 B4		Veronica Clo. LN4	15 C2
The Paddock,			Vicarage Dri. LN6	16 C5
Sudbrooke. LN2	17 B3		Vicarage La. LN2	16 C2
The Parade. LN3	4 B4		Vicars Ct. LN2	5 C2
The Rowans. LN2	16 B2		Victor Dri. LN6	12 B4
The Sidings. LN6	5 A4		Victor Way. LN5	17 C5
The Steepers. LN2	16 D1		Victoria Gro. LN4	14 D2
Theodore St. LN1	5 A1		Victoria Pass. LN1	5 A2
Thesiger St. LN5	10 C2		Victoria St,	
Thirlmere Clo. LN6	13 E4		Bracebridge. LN5	10 B6
Thirlmere Way. LN6	8 C2		Victoria St,	
Thirsk Dri. LN6	12 D2		Lincoln. LN1	5 B2
Thistle Clo. LN2	7 F1		Victoria Ter. LN1	5 A2
Thomas St. LN2	5 E3		Viking Clo. LN5	17 B5
Thonock Clo. LN6	6 C3		Villa Clo. LN4	15 D3
Thoresby Clo. LN5	13 H5		Vine St. LN2	5 D2
Thoresway Dri. LN2	6 D2		Vulcan Cres. LN6	12 B4
			Vulcan Dri. LN1	17 C5

Waddingworth Gro. LN2	6 D1	Welbeck St. LN2	5 F3
Wainer Clo. LN6	8 C6	Welbourn Gdns. LN2	6 D2
Wake St. LN1	6 B4	Well La. LN2	5 C2
Wakefield Clo. LN4	15 C4	Welland Rd. LN1	6 A2
Walbury Clo. LN5	13 H3	Wellingore Rd. LN2	6 B1
Walcot Clo. LN6	9 E5	Wellington Clo. LN1	16 B4
Waldeck St. LN1	6 B4	Wellington Sq. LN5	17 D6
Waldo Rd. LN4	10 C6	Wellington St. LN1	6 A5
Walford Dri. LN6	9 F5	Wells Clo. LN4	14 E2
Wallis Av. LN6	13 F2	Wells Rd. LN4	15 C4
Walmer St. LN2	7 F6	Wellsykes La. LN4	14 A4
Walnut Clo. LN5	13 G5	Welton Gdns. LN2	6 D1
Walnut Pl. LN5	10 C2	Welton Rd. LN2	16 A2
Waltham Clo. LN6	8 B5	Wentworth Clo. LN4	14 E2
Waltham Rd. LN6	8 B5	West Dri. LN2	17 B1
Wasdale Clo. LN6	8 C2	West Millgate. LN3	4 B5
Washdyke La, Bracebridge		West Par. LN1	5 A2
Low Fields. LN6	13 F6	Westbourne Gro. LN1	6 B6
Washdyke La,		Westbrooke Clo. LN6	9 G4
Nettleham. LN2	16 A2	Westbrooke Rd. LN6	9 G4
Washingborough Rd,		Westcliffe St. LN1	6 B3
Canwick. LN5	10 D3	Western Av,	
Washingborough Rd,		Boultham Moor. LN6	9 G4
Heighington. LN4	14 C3	Western Av,	
Water La, Lincoln. LN1	5 B3	Bracebridge Heath. LN4	15 B5
Water La,		Western Cres. LN6	9 G4
North Hykeham. LN6	12 D5	Westfield La. LN2	4 A2
Waterford La. LN3	4 A5	Westfield St. LN1	6 A6
Waterloo La. LN6	16 C6	Westgate. LN1	5 B1
Waterloo St. LN6	10 A2	Westholm. LN3	4 B6
Watermill La. LN2	16 B2	Westholm Clo. LN2	7 F2
Waterside North. LN2	5 B3	Westminster Dri. LN4	15 C4
Waterside Shopping		*Westminster Ho,	
Centre. LN2	5 C3	Weldon Gdns. LN2	6 D1
Waterside South. LN5	5 C4	Westminster Rd. LN6	12 B2
Watling Clo. LN4	15 C6	Westway. LN2	16.C2
Wavell Dri. LN3	7 G6	Westwick Dri. LN6	9 G5
Wavell Rd. LN3	7 G6	Westwick Gdns. LN6	9 G6
Waverley Av. LN6	12 D2	Westwood Clo. LN6	9 F3
Webb St. LN1	10 B3	Westwood Dri. LN6	9 F3
Webster Clo. LN6	9 F6	Wetherby Cres. LN6	12 D2
Wedgewood Clo. LN6	8 C4	Weymouth Clo. LN5	13 H3
Wedgewood Gro. LN6	8 C4	Wharfedale Dri. LN6	13 E3
Wedgewood Rd. LN6	8 C4	Wheatfield Rd. LN6	8 B2
Weir St. LN5	10 B4	Wheelwright La. LN4	14 E4

Whisby Rd. LN6	12 A1	Woburn Av. LN1	6
Whisby Way. LN6	12 B1	Wold View. LN3	16
Whitehall Cres. LN4	15 B4	Wolsey Way. LN2	7
Whitehall Gro. LN1	5 A3	Woodbank. LN6	16
Whitethorn Gro. LN6	8 B2	Woodburn Clo. LN1	6
Whitley Clo. LN6	16 B5	*Woodburn Vw,	
Wickenby Clo. LN6	13 E2	Woodburn Clo. LN1	6
Wickenby Cres. LN1	6 B2	Woodfield Av. LN6	8
Wigford Way. LN1	5 B3	Woodfield Ct. LN6	8
Wigsley Clo. LN6	8 C6	Woodhall Dri. LN2	6
Wigsley Rd. LN6	8 C6	Woodland Av. LN6	16
Williamson St. LN1	6 C4	Woodland View. LN2	5
Willingham Av. LN2	6 C2	Woodpecker Clo. LN6	16
Willis Clo. LN1	5 A1	Woodrush Rd. LN2	7
Willoughby La. LN5	13 G4	Woodside. LN4	15
Willow Ct,		*Woodside Ct,	
Bracebridge Heath. LN4	15 C6	Nightingale Cres. LN6	8
Willow Ct,		Woodstock St. LN1	6
Washingborough. LN4	14 C1	Woodvale Clo. LN6	8
Willow Rd, Branston. LN4	15 B1	Woodvale Cres. LN6	8
Willow Rd,		Woolley Rd. LN2	17
North Hykeham. LN6	12 D3	Worcester Clo,	
Willow Tree Gdns. LN6	8 C3	Birchwood. LN6	8
Willowfield Av. LN2	16 D2	Worcester Clo,	
Wilson St. LN1	6 B4	Bracebridge Heath. LN4	15
Winchester Clo. LN4	15 C4	Wordsworth St. LN1	5
Winchester Dri. LN4	14 C2	Wragby Rd,	
Windermere Av. LN6	13 E4	Lincoln. LN2	5
Windermere Rd. LN2	7 F1	Wragby Rd,	
Windmill View. LN1	6 B4	Sudbrooke. LN2	17
Windsor Clo. LN4	17 B2	Wragby Rd East. LN2	4
Windsor Park Clo. LN6	13 E5	Wrightsway. LN2	7
Winn St. LN2	5 E3	Wroxham Clo. LN6	13
Winniffe Gdns. LN2	7 G2	Wyatt Rd. LN5	10
Winnowsty La. LN2	5 D1	Wyton Clo. LN6	8
Winster Clo. LN2	6 D1	Wyvill Walk. LN6	9
Winthorpe Clo. LN6	8 C5	Yale Clo. LN4	14
Winthorpe Gro. LN6	8 C5	Yarborough Cres. LN1	6
Winthorpe Rd. LN6	8 C5	Yarborough Rd. LN1	5
Wiseholme Rd. LN6	16 C6	Yarborough Ter. LN1	5
Wisteria Av. LN4	15 B1	Yates Clo. LN2	7
Witchford Clo. LN6	8 B5	York Av. LN1	6
Witchford Rd. LN6	8 B5	York Clo. LN4	14
Witham View. LN4	14 A1		
Wittering Clo. LN6	8 C5		